Chucks Feeney:

Lessons in Impactful Giving

Jerry C. Smith

Lesson in impactful giving

"Chuck Feeney: Lessons in Impactful Giving"

TABLE OF CONTENTS

INTRODUCTION:

CHAPTER 1:WHO IS CHUCKS FEENEY:

1.1:Humble Beginnings:

1.2:Early Life:

1.3:Family Background:

1.4:Educational Journey:

1.5:Early Career:

CHAPTER 2:The Birth of Duty-Free Shoppers:

2.1:Co-founding DFS:

2.2:Shaping the Travel Retail Industry:

2.3:Entrepreneurial Successes:

2.4:Challenges:

CHAPTER 3:The Quiet Philanthropist:

3.1:Approach to Giving:

3.2:Fulfilment of the Giving Pledge:

3.3:A Pioneering Example:

3.4:The Beginnings of The Atlantic

Philanthropies:

CHAPTER 4:Visionary Giving:

4.1:Funding Higher Education:

4.2:Medical Research:

4.3:Advancing Social Justice:

4.4:Human Rights:

4.5:Global Impact of His Philanthropy:

CHAPTER 5:The Art of Giving While Living:

Lesson in impactful giving

5.1:The Decision to Give Away His

Wealth During His Lifetime:

5.2:Fulfilling a Vision:

5.3:Philanthropic Principles:

5.4:Strategies:

CHAPTER 6:The Secret Billionaire:

No

6.1:The Remarkable Secrecy

Surrounding Feeney's Philanthropy:

6.2:Legacy of Anonymous Giving:

6.3:A Lesson in Selflessness:

6.4:The Billionaire Who Lived Frugally:

CHAPTER 7:Philanthropy's Endgame:

7.1:The Final Contributions:

7.2:Dissolution of The Atlantic Philanthropies:

7.3:The Legacy of Chuck Feeney's Giving:

7.4:Inspiring Future Generations:

CHAPTER 8:Impact on Society:

8.1:Examining the Enduring Impact of Chuck Feeney's Philanthropy:

8.2:Social Justice and Equality:

8.3:Challenging Discrimination:

8.4:Lessons for Aspiring Philanthropists:

CHAPTER 9:Life Beyond Philanthropy:

Lesson in impactful giving

9.1:Retirement:

9.2:Personal Life:

9.3:Reflecting on a Life of Purpose:

9.4:Lessons for Future Generations:

CONCLUSION:

Lesson in impactful giving

Lesson in impactful giving

Lesson in impactful giving

INTRODUCTION:

"Chuck Feeney: Lessons in Impactful Giving"

In a world often defined by wealth accumulation and opulence, there exist individuals whose life stories stand as a testament to the transformative power of selfless generosity. Chuck Feeney, a name that may not have always graced the front pages of tabloids or financial magazines, embodies a unique and inspiring narrative—one that revolves around the art of impactful giving.

The pages of this book will unveil the extraordinary journey of Charles "Chuck" Feeney, a man whose remarkable life has not only redefined the concepts of wealth and philanthropy but has left an indelible mark on society. With a legacy that champions the ideals of humility, frugality, and a relentless commitment to improving the lives of others, Chuck Feeney serves as a beacon of hope and inspiration in our complex world.

This book will delve into the life of a visionary entrepreneur, who, despite co-founding a pioneering empire in the travel retail industry, chose to live a life that was anything but conventional. Chuck Feeney's story is one of contrasts—a billionaire who deliberately lived without the trappings of immense wealth, and a man who believed in the concept of "giving while living," thus reshaping the landscape of modern philanthropy.

Through his quiet yet profound acts of charity and a commitment to address pressing global issues, Chuck Feeney has rewritten the rulebook on what it means to be a philanthropist. His unwavering dedication to causes ranging from education and healthcare to social justice and human rights has had an unparalleled impact on countless lives, transcending borders and generations.

As we embark on this journey through Chuck Feeney's life, we will uncover the principles that underpinned his approach to impactful giving. We will explore the motivations that drove him to lead a life of purpose, as well as the lessons he leaves behind for aspiring philanthropists and individuals who seek to make a meaningful difference in the world.

"Chuck Feeney: Lessons in Impactful Giving" is not just a biography but a testament to the idea that one person's commitment to making the world a better place can resonate far beyond their own lifetime. It is an exploration of the transformative power of generosity, humility, and the enduring impact of a life lived with purpose.

CHAPTER 1:WHO IS CHUCKS FEENEY:

Charles Francis Chuck Feeney is an Irish-American businessman, philanthropist, and founder of The Atlantic Philanthropies, one of the largest and most secretive philanthropic foundations in the world. Born on April 23, 1931, in Elizabeth, New Jersey, Chuck Feeney is best known for his remarkable commitment to philanthropy and his philosophy of "giving while living.

Key points about Chuck Feeney include:

1. Co-founder of Duty-Free Shoppers (DFS): Feeney made his fortune through the co-founding of Duty-Free Shoppers, a pioneering company in the travel retail industry. DFS transformed the way people shop for luxury goods at airports and border crossings.

2. Frugal Lifestyle:Despite amassing great wealth, Chuck Feeney chose to lead a frugal and unostentatious

lifestyle. He lived in a modest apartment, wore simple clothing, and flew economy class.

3. The Secret Billionaire: For much of his life, Feeney kept his philanthropic activities a closely guarded secret. He donated large sums of money anonymously and went to great lengths to avoid public recognition.

4. Giving While Living:Chuck Feeney is known for his commitment to "giving while living." Instead of waiting to bequeath his wealth through a foundation after his death, he actively gave away his fortune during his lifetime to a wide range of causes and organisations.

5. The Atlantic Philanthropies: Feeney founded The Atlantic Philanthropies in 1982 as a vehicle for his philanthropic efforts. Over the years, the foundation has donated billions of dollars to causes such as education, healthcare, social justice, and human rights, with a particular focus on Ireland and the United States.

6. Impactful Giving:Chuck Feeney's philanthropy has had a transformative impact on various sectors, including higher education. His contributions have funded research, scholarships, and infrastructure development in universities and institutions around the world.

7. Awards and Recognition: In recognition of his remarkable philanthropic work, Chuck Feeney has received numerous awards and honours, including being named one of "The World's 50 Greatest Leaders" by Fortune magazine.

8. End of Giving:In 2020, Chuck Feeney fulfilled his goal of giving away his entire fortune and officially closed The Atlantic Philanthropies. This act marked the end of an era in philanthropy.

Chuck Feeney's story is one of humility, extraordinary generosity, and a deep commitment to making the world a better place. His life's work has left an enduring legacy, inspiring others to think creatively and compassionately about the impact of their wealth on society.

1.1:Humble Beginnings:

Chuck Feeney's remarkable journey from humble beginnings to becoming one of the world's most influential philanthropists is a testament to the power of determination and purpose. Born on April 23, 1931, in Elizabeth, New Jersey, Chuck Feeney's early life was marked by modesty and the values that would shape his future.

1. A Modest Upbringing:

Chuck Feeney was the son of Irish-American parents. His father, a firefighter, and his mother, a nurse, instilled in him the values of hard work, frugality, and the importance of education from a young age. These values would become central to his life and philanthropic endeavours.

2. The GI Bill and Education:

After serving in the U.S. Air Force during the Korean War, Chuck Feeney used the G.I. Bill to pursue higher education. He attended Cornell University, where he studied hotel management. It was during his time at Cornell that he met Robert Miller, with whom he would later co-found Duty-Free Shoppers (DFS).

3. The Birth of Duty-Free Shoppers:

In 1960, Chuck Feeney and Robert Miller co-founded Duty-Free Shoppers, a company that would revolutionise the travel retail industry. They began by selling duty-free liquor and cigarettes to American servicemen in East Asia. This venture laid the foundation for their future success.

4. Entrepreneurial Success:

Duty-Free Shoppers expanded rapidly, capitalising on the growing trend of international travel. The company's concept of offering luxury goods at duty-free prices at airports and border crossings was groundbreaking and highly profitable.

5. A Simple and Unassuming Lifestyle:

Despite accumulating great wealth through DFS, Chuck Feeney chose to live a life of simplicity and frugality. He lived in a modest apartment, avoided luxury possessions, and flew economy class. This lifestyle allowed him to allocate the majority of his wealth to philanthropic endeavors.

6. A Commitment to "Giving While Living":

Chuck Feeney's early experiences and values guided him toward a philanthropic approach known as "giving while living." Rather than waiting to leave a bequest through a foundation after his death, he was determined to use his wealth to make a positive impact during his lifetime.

Chuck Feeney's humble beginnings and the values instilled in him during his upbringing were instrumental in shaping his philanthropic journey. His commitment to improving the lives of others and his dedication to causes ranging from education and healthcare to social justice and human rights have left an enduring legacy of generosity and compassion. His story serves as an inspiration to individuals from all walks of life, reminding us that the impact of one person's actions can transcend circumstances and transform the world.Chuck Feeney's commitment to "giving while living" is a defining principle that distinguishes him as a philanthropist of extraordinary vision and impact. While many individuals and foundations choose to allocate their wealth posthumously, Feeney embraced a radically different approach—one that emphasized the urgency and immediacy of addressing pressing global challenges during his lifetime.

1. The Philanthropic Philosophy:

Feeney's philosophy of "giving while living" was rooted in a deep sense of responsibility and a desire to see the tangible impact of his wealth. He believed that one's wealth should not be hoarded but should serve as a force for positive change in the world, addressing critical issues such as education, healthcare, social justice, and human rights.

2. Anonymity and Humility:

Perhaps one of the most remarkable aspects of Chuck Feeney's philanthropy was his commitment to anonymity. For many years, he gave away vast sums of money anonymously, striving to avoid public recognition. He believed that true giving should be devoid of personal gain or acclaim.

3. The Atlantic Philanthropies:

In 1982, Chuck Feeney established The Atlantic Philanthropies as the vehicle for his philanthropic efforts. Over the decades, this foundation became one of the world's largest, supporting a wide range of causes and initiatives. The foundation's motto, "Expenditure Down, Invest Up," exemplified Feeney's determination to donate his fortune actively.

4. Funding Transformational Change:

Through The Atlantic Philanthropies, Chuck Feeney funded projects and organisations that aimed not only to alleviate suffering but also to create transformative, long-lasting change. His investments in higher education, healthcare research, and human rights advocacy have had a profound and enduring impact.

5. Giving It All Away:

Chuck Feeney was unwavering in his commitment to giving away his entire fortune. He set a clear goal to "die broke," ensuring that his wealth was used for the greater good rather than accumulating for personal gain or inheritance.

6. Closing The Atlantic Philanthropies:

In 2020, Chuck Feeney fulfilled his promise by officially closing The Atlantic Philanthropies. By this time, he had donated over $8 billion to causes around the world. This marked the end of one of the most remarkable philanthropic journeys in history.

7. An Enduring Legacy:

Chuck Feeney's commitment to "giving while living" leaves behind a legacy of profound impact and inspiration. His approach challenges conventional notions of wealth and encourages individuals of means to be active and deliberate stewards of their resources.

Chuck Feeney's philanthropic journey demonstrates that it is not the accumulation of wealth but the meaningful and purposeful deployment of it that defines a life's true success. His commitment to addressing societal issues head-on, his humility, and his belief in the power of immediate action serve as a powerful model for philanthropists and individuals alike, inspiring us to use our resources and influence to create positive change in the world, not someday, but today.

1.2:Early Life:

Chuck Feeney's early life provides a crucial backdrop to understanding the man who would go on to become one of the world's most influential philanthropists. His upbringing, experiences, and values instilled during his formative years played a pivotal role in shaping his future endeavours.

1. Humble Beginnings in New Jersey:

Charles Francis Feeney, born on April 23, 1931, in Elizabeth, New Jersey, came into the world during a time of economic uncertainty, growing up amid the challenges of the Great Depression. His family's modest circumstances would later influence his outlook on wealth and success.

2. Irish-American Heritage:

Feeney's family had strong Irish-American roots, and this heritage was an important part of his identity. The values of hard work, frugality, and resilience, often associated with Irish-American culture, were passed down to him.

3. A Focus on Education:

Chuck Feeney's parents recognized the value of education and encouraged him to excel academically. His early experiences in school laid the foundation for his future academic pursuits.

4. Military Service and the G.I. Bill:

After completing high school, Chuck Feeney enlisted in the U.S. Air Force during the Korean War. His military service exposed him to different cultures and provided opportunities for personal growth. Importantly, he utilised the G.I. Bill to fund his higher education, a decision that would prove pivotal.

5. Cornell University and the Birth of DFS:

Feeney attended Cornell University, where he pursued studies in hotel management. It was at Cornell that he met Robert Miller, a fellow student who would become his business partner. Together, they founded Duty-Free Shoppers (DFS), a venture that would eventually bring them great wealth.

6. Early Entrepreneurial Spirit:

Even before DFS, Chuck Feeney demonstrated an entrepreneurial spirit. He engaged in various business endeavours during his youth, including selling Christmas cards and magazines.

7. Values of Frugality and Humility:

Throughout his early life, Chuck Feeney's parents instilled in him values of frugality and humility. These values would become central to his identity and influence his approach to wealth and philanthropy.

Chuck Feeney's early life experiences, marked by a modest upbringing, a commitment to education, and the values of hard work and humility, laid the groundwork for his future achievements. These formative years helped shape the man who would later become a pioneer in philanthropy, known for his commitment to "giving while living" and his dedication to using his wealth to make the world a better place.

1.3:Family Background:

Chuck Feeney's family background played a significant role in shaping his values, work ethic, and approach to life. Born into a modest Irish-American family, his upbringing instilled in him core principles that would later guide his remarkable philanthropic journey.

1. Irish-American Heritage:

Chuck Feeney's family had deep Irish-American roots. This heritage was an important part of his identity, and he often spoke fondly of his Irish ancestry. The values of resilience, community, and strong family bonds commonly associated with Irish-American culture had a lasting impact on him.

2. Modest Upbringing:

Chuck was raised in a working-class neighborhood in Elizabeth, New Jersey. His parents, a firefighter and a nurse, provided for their family through hard work and dedication. Growing up in a household where resources were limited, Chuck learned the value of making the most of what one had.

3. Emphasis on Education:

Despite their modest means, Chuck's parents recognized the importance of education. They encouraged him and his siblings to excel academically and saw education as a pathway to greater opportunities.

4. Strong Work Ethic:

Chuck's father, a firefighter, exemplified a strong work ethic through his commitment to public service. This work ethic was passed down to Chuck and became a defining trait throughout his life.

5. Sense of Community:

The close-knit Irish-American community in which Chuck grew up fostered a sense of belonging and solidarity. This sense of community would later influence his philanthropic approach, emphasising the importance of giving back and supporting those in need.

6. Humility and Frugality:

Perhaps the most enduring values instilled in Chuck by his family were humility and frugality. His parents led by example, living simple, modest lives despite any financial success they achieved. These values left an indelible mark on Chuck, shaping his decision to live a life of minimal material excess even when he became incredibly wealthy.

Chuck Feeney's family background, characterised by strong Irish-American values, a focus on education, a commitment to hard work, and an unwavering dedication to humility and frugality, provided the foundation for his philanthropic journey. These values became the driving force behind his desire to make a positive impact on the world, emphasising the importance of using one's resources to benefit others.

1.4:Educational Journey:

Chuck Feeney's educational journey played a pivotal role in shaping his life and eventual success as an entrepreneur and philanthropist. From his early academic pursuits to his commitment to lifelong learning, education remained a cornerstone of his personal and professional development.

1. Early Education:

Chuck Feeney's educational journey began in his hometown of Elizabeth, New Jersey, where he attended local schools. His parents, recognizing the value of education, encouraged him to excel academically.

2. Service in the U.S. Air Force:

Following high school, Chuck enlisted in the U.S. Air Force during the Korean War. His military service not only exposed him to different cultures and experiences but also provided him with valuable life skills and opportunities for personal growth.

3. Utilising the G.I. Bill:

Chuck Feeney's decision to leverage the benefits of the G.I. Bill marked a significant turning point in his educational journey. This program provided financial assistance for veterans' education, enabling him to pursue higher studies.

4. Cornell University:

Feeney enrolled at Cornell University in Ithaca, New York, where he studied hotel management. It was during his time at Cornell that he crossed paths with Robert Miller, a fellow student who would later become his business partner in the creation of Duty-Free Shoppers (DFS).

5. Entrepreneurial Spirit:

Even during his college years, Chuck Feeney demonstrated an entrepreneurial spirit. He engaged in various business ventures, including selling Christmas cards and magazines, which hinted at his future success as an entrepreneur.

6. Lifelong Learning:

Throughout his life, Chuck Feeney maintained a commitment to lifelong learning. He understood that education extended beyond the classroom and encompassed experiences, reading, and exposure to diverse perspectives.

7. Philanthropic Investment in Education:

Chuck Feeney's dedication to education extended to his philanthropic efforts. He generously supported educational institutions around the world, funding scholarships, research, and infrastructure development in universities and schools.

8. The Power of Knowledge:

Chuck Feeney believed deeply in the power of knowledge and education as tools for personal growth and societal progress. His experiences, both in formal education and in the world, informed his philanthropic endeavours and the causes he chose to support.

Chuck Feeney's educational journey is a testament to his belief in the transformative potential of learning and the importance of investing in one's own intellectual development. His commitment to education, both as a means of personal advancement and as a vehicle for creating positive change in society, became a central theme in his philanthropic legacy.

1.5:Early Career:

Chuck Feeney's early career marked the beginning of a remarkable journey that would eventually lead him to become a successful entrepreneur and philanthropist. His experiences in business, particularly the founding of Duty-Free Shoppers (DFS), laid the foundation for his later philanthropic endeavours.

1. Duty-Free Shoppers (DFS):

Chuck Feeney's early career breakthrough came with the founding of Duty-Free Shoppers (DFS). Alongside his college friend Robert Miller, Feeney established DFS in 1960.

DFS was initially focused on selling duty-free liquor and cigarettes to U.S. military personnel stationed in East Asia. This venture capitalized on the growing trend of international travel and the demand for duty-free products.

The innovative concept of offering luxury goods at duty-free prices at airports and border crossings proved to be a game-changer in the travel retail industry.

2. Pioneering Travel Retail:

Chuck Feeney's vision for DFS transformed the way people shopped for luxury goods while travelling. DFS stores became iconic destinations at airports worldwide.

The success of DFS was instrumental in shaping the travel retail industry, and the company played a pivotal role in making duty-free shopping a global phenomenon.

3. Expansion and Success:

DFS expanded rapidly, capitalising on the increasing volume of international travel. The company's ability to adapt and innovate contributed to its success.

Chuck Feeney's business acumen and commitment to providing high-quality products and service were key factors in DFS's growth and profitability.

4. Ethical Business Practices:

Throughout his career, Feeney adhered to a set of ethical principles that emphasised fairness, transparency, and integrity in business dealings. These values would later inform his philanthropic work.

5. Accumulation of Wealth:

The success of DFS led to the accumulation of significant wealth for Chuck Feeney and his business partner Robert Miller.

6. Commitment to Frugality:

Despite amassing considerable wealth, Feeney's personal lifestyle remained notably modest. He lived in a simple apartment, avoided luxury possessions, and chose to fly economy class.

7. The Birth of Philanthropic Ideals:

Chuck Feeney's early career experiences sowed the seeds of his philanthropic ideals. As he became wealthier, he began to contemplate how he could use his fortune for the greater good.

Chuck Feeney's early career in business, particularly his pioneering role in the travel retail industry with DFS, set the stage for his later philanthropic journey. The success of DFS provided him with the resources and influence to make a profound impact on society through his commitment to "giving while living" and his unwavering dedication to addressing global challenges.

CHAPTER 2:The Birth of Duty-Free Shoppers:

The birth of Duty-Free Shoppers (DFS) represents a pivotal moment in Chuck Feeney's life and in the evolution of the travel retail industry. It was the visionary creation of DFS that catapulted Chuck Feeney into the world of entrepreneurship and eventually laid the groundwork for his extraordinary philanthropic journey.

1. Early Entrepreneurial Ventures:

Chuck Feeney's journey into business began with small entrepreneurial ventures during his youth. He displayed a knack for spotting opportunities and a drive for success.

2. Meeting Robert Miller:

While attending Cornell University, Chuck Feeney met Robert Miller, a fellow student. Their friendship would prove instrumental in shaping the future of the travel retail industry.

3. Identifying a Unique Opportunity:

Feeney and Miller noticed a unique opportunity during a trip to Europe. They observed the growing trend of international travel and recognized that travellers had a desire for duty-free goods.

4. Founding Duty-Free Shoppers (DFS):

In 1960, Chuck Feeney and Robert Miller co-founded Duty-Free Shoppers. Their goal was to create a retail concept that would cater to travelers by offering luxury goods at duty-free prices.

The first DFS store opened in Hong Kong, targeting American military personnel stationed in Asia.

5. Innovative Retail Concept:

DFS revolutionised the retail industry by introducing the concept of duty-free shopping. Travellers could purchase high-end products such as liquor, perfume, and cigarettes without paying import duties.

The success of DFS was built on the idea of providing a unique shopping experience to travellers, making their journeys more enjoyable and economical.

6. Rapid Expansion:

The concept of duty-free shopping proved immensely popular, and DFS expanded rapidly. New stores were established in strategic locations, including airports and border crossings.

The company's adaptability and focus on customer satisfaction contributed to its growth and global reach.

7. DFS Legacy:

Duty-Free Shoppers became synonymous with high-quality, tax-free shopping. It played a crucial role in shaping the travel retail industry and remains a prominent presence at airports and other travel hubs worldwide.

8. Wealth Accumulation and Philanthropic Vision:

The success of DFS led to the accumulation of substantial wealth for Chuck Feeney and Robert Miller.

It was during this period that Feeney began to formulate his philanthropic ideals, setting the stage for his later commitment to "giving while living."

The birth of Duty-Free Shoppers represented not only a groundbreaking business venture but also the beginning of Chuck Feeney's exploration of how wealth and success could be used to benefit society. DFS's innovative approach to retailing and its global impact foreshadowed Feeney's future philanthropic efforts, which would leave an enduring mark on the world.Chuck Feeney's wealth accumulation and the development of his philanthropic vision are integral parts of his remarkable life story. As he achieved substantial success through Duty-Free Shoppers (DFS), he began to formulate the principles that would guide his extraordinary commitment to philanthropy and giving while living.

1. DFS's Global Success:

Duty-Free Shoppers (DFS) achieved remarkable success and rapid expansion, thanks to its innovative concept of duty-free shopping at airports and border crossings. The company's global reach brought Chuck Feeney considerable wealth.

2. Accumulation of Substantial Wealth:

As DFS flourished, Chuck Feeney's personal wealth grew significantly. This period marked a turning point in his life, prompting him to consider the responsibility that came with great affluence.

3. Transition to Philanthropy:

Chuck Feeney's transition from wealth accumulation to philanthropy was driven by a deep sense of responsibility and a desire to make a meaningful impact on society. He believed that his wealth could be a force for good.

4. Commitment to "Giving While Living":

One of the central tenets of Chuck Feeney's philanthropic vision was the idea of "giving while living." Rather than waiting to leave a bequest through a foundation after his death, he was committed to actively and intentionally giving away his fortune during his lifetime.

5. Anonymity and Humility:

Feeney's approach to philanthropy was characterised by humility and a desire for anonymity. He believed that true giving should be devoid of personal recognition or gain. For many years, he gave away vast sums of money anonymously.

6. The Atlantic Philanthropies:

In 1982, Chuck Feeney established The Atlantic Philanthropies as the vehicle for his philanthropic efforts. The foundation was designed to support a wide range of causes and initiatives, with a focus on creating positive change in society.

7. Areas of Focus:

The Atlantic Philanthropies funded projects and organisations in various sectors, including education, healthcare, social justice, human rights, and peace-building. Chuck Feeney's philanthropy aimed not only to alleviate suffering but also to address systemic issues and create lasting impact.

8. Closing The Atlantic Philanthropies:

In 2020, Chuck Feeney fulfilled his goal of giving away his entire fortune. He officially closed The Atlantic Philanthropies, marking the end of an era in philanthropy. His act of "giving while living" had a profound impact on countless lives.

Chuck Feeney's wealth accumulation and philanthropic vision serve as a testament to the transformative potential of wealth when used with wisdom, compassion, and a commitment to making the world a better place. His dedication to giving away his fortune during his lifetime and his emphasis on humility and anonymity continue to inspire individuals and philanthropists around the world, challenging them to think beyond personal gain and leave a lasting legacy of positive change.

2.1:Co-founding DFS:

Chuck Feeney's founding of Duty-Free Shoppers (DFS) marked the beginning of a remarkable entrepreneurial journey that would eventually lead him to become one of the world's most influential philanthropists. His vision and dedication played a pivotal role in revolutionising the travel retail industry.

1. Identifying a Unique Opportunity:

Chuck Feeney and his college friend Robert Miller recognized a unique opportunity in the growing trend of international travel. They saw that travelers desired access to high-quality products without the burden of import duties.

2. Co-Founding Duty-Free Shoppers (DFS):

In 1960, Chuck Feeney and Robert Miller co-founded Duty-Free Shoppers (DFS). Their goal was to create a retail concept that would cater to travellers by offering luxury goods at duty-free prices.

3. The Inaugural DFS Store in Hong Kong:

The first DFS store opened in Hong Kong, targeting American military personnel stationed in Asia. This location proved to be strategically important for the success of DFS.

4. Innovative Retail Concept:

DFS introduced a groundbreaking concept in retail by providing travellers the opportunity to purchase high-end products, such as liquor, perfume, and cigarettes, at duty-free prices. This concept transformed the way people shopped while travelling.

5. Expanding the DFS Brand:

DFS expanded rapidly, opening stores in key locations, including airports and border crossings. The company's adaptability and focus on customer satisfaction contributed to its growth and global reach.

6. Shaping the Travel Retail Industry:

DFS played a pivotal role in shaping the travel retail industry. Chuck Feeney's vision for DFS made duty-free shopping a global phenomenon, and DFS became synonymous with high-quality, tax-free shopping.

7. Commitment to Excellence:

Throughout DFS's growth and success, Chuck Feeney maintained a commitment to excellence, ensuring that customers received top-notch products and service.

8. Legacy of Innovation:

Chuck Feeney's innovative approach to retailing and his dedication to providing travellers with a unique shopping experience left a lasting legacy. DFS became a prominent presence at airports and other travel hubs worldwide.

9. Philanthropic Beginnings:

The wealth generated from the success of DFS laid the foundation for Chuck Feeney's later philanthropic endeavours. His experiences in business and entrepreneurship inspired his commitment to "giving while living."

Chuck Feeney's founding of Duty-Free Shoppers exemplified his entrepreneurial spirit and ability to identify opportunities for positive disruption. The success of DFS not only transformed the retail landscape but also set the stage for Feeney's incredible philanthropic journey, where he would use his wealth to create lasting change in the world.

2.2:Shaping the Travel Retail Industry:

Chuck Feeney's role in shaping the travel retail industry through the creation of Duty-Free Shoppers (DFS) is a testament to his visionary approach to business. DFS not only revolutionised the way people shop while travelling but also set industry standards and left an indelible mark on the travel retail landscape.

1. Introduction of the Duty-Free Concept:
   Chuck Feeney and his partner Robert Miller introduced the concept of duty-free shopping, allowing travellers to

purchase high-quality products without paying import duties or taxes.

This innovative approach addressed a critical need for travellers who sought access to luxury goods at more affordable prices.

2. The First DFS Store:

The first DFS store opened in Hong Kong in 1960. This strategic location, with its proximity to American military personnel stationed in Asia, laid the foundation for DFS's success.

3. Rapid Expansion:

Recognizing the demand for duty-free shopping, DFS expanded rapidly. Stores were strategically located at airports and border crossings, ensuring maximum exposure to travellers.

This expansion contributed significantly to the growth of the travel retail industry.

4. Transforming the Shopping Experience:

DFS set a new standard for the travel retail experience. The stores were designed to provide an enjoyable and convenient shopping environment for travellers.

Travellers could explore a wide range of luxury products, from perfumes and cosmetics to liquor and tobacco, all without the burden of customs duties.

5. Global Presence:

DFS's global reach extended to airports and destinations worldwide. The brand became synonymous with high-quality, tax-free shopping.

DFS stores became iconic destinations for travellers, enhancing their overall travel experience.

6. Fostering Innovation:

Chuck Feeney's commitment to excellence and innovation influenced the entire travel retail industry. DFS's success encouraged other companies to improve their offerings and services to cater to travellers' needs.

7. Industry Standards and Practices:

DFS's practices and commitment to customer satisfaction set industry standards. Competitors and newcomers in the travel retail sector often looked to DFS as a model of success.

8. Legacy in Travel Retail:

Chuck Feeney's contribution to shaping the travel retail industry through DFS left a lasting legacy. Duty-free shopping continues to be a significant part of the travel experience for millions of travelers worldwide.

Chuck Feeney's innovative approach to retailing and his dedication to providing travellers with a unique and enjoyable shopping experience reshaped the travel retail industry. DFS's success not only enriched his life but also provided the resources and inspiration for his later philanthropic journey, which focused on improving lives and making a positive impact on a global scale.

2.3:Entrepreneurial Successes:

Chuck Feeney's entrepreneurial successes are a testament to his innovative spirit, vision, and determination. His career spanned various ventures, but it was his co-founding of Duty-Free Shoppers (DFS) that catapulted him to international prominence as a successful entrepreneur.

1. Duty-Free Shoppers (DFS):
   Chuck Feeney and his college friend Robert Miller co-founded Duty-Free Shoppers in 1960. This innovative venture introduced the concept of duty-free shopping to travellers, allowing them to purchase luxury goods at tax-free prices.
   DFS's unique approach revolutionised the travel retail industry and set new standards for shopping experiences at airports and border crossings.

2. Pioneering a Retail Revolution:
   DFS's introduction of duty-free shopping was a game-changer in the retail industry. It transformed the

way people shopped while travelling and tapped into the growing trend of international tourism.

3. Rapid Expansion:

Chuck Feeney's leadership and business acumen contributed to DFS's rapid expansion. The company opened stores at key travel hubs worldwide, from airports to cruise terminals, ensuring a global presence.

4. Setting Industry Standards:

DFS's commitment to customer service, quality products, and a luxurious shopping experience set industry standards for travel retail. Competitors looked to DFS as a benchmark for excellence.

5. Wealth Accumulation:

The success of DFS led to significant wealth accumulation for Chuck Feeney and his partner Robert Miller. This financial success provided the resources for his later philanthropic endeavors.

6. Ethical Business Practices:

Throughout his entrepreneurial career, Feeney adhered to ethical business practices. He valued fairness, transparency, and integrity in all his dealings, setting a high moral standard for his ventures.

7. Commitment to Giving Back:

As his wealth grew, Chuck Feeney's commitment to philanthropy became increasingly evident. He transitioned from a focus on wealth accumulation to a dedication to "giving while living."

8. A Model for Philanthropy:

Chuck Feeney's journey from entrepreneurial success to pioneering philanthropy serves as a model for others. His approach challenged conventional notions of wealth and encouraged active and impactful giving.

Chuck Feeney's entrepreneurial successes, particularly his role in founding DFS, reshaped the retail industry and left a lasting legacy. His commitment to ethical business practices, innovation, and philanthropy not only benefited him personally but also had a profound impact on the lives of countless individuals and communities worldwide.Chuck Feeney's commitment to giving back is a defining feature of his life and legacy. As he accumulated wealth through successful ventures like Duty-Free Shoppers (DFS), he transitioned from a focus on personal gain to a profound dedication to philanthropy. His commitment to "giving while living" has had a transformative impact on numerous causes and organisations around the world.

1. A Shift in Priorities:

As Chuck Feeney's wealth grew, he experienced a fundamental shift in his priorities. He recognized the responsibility that came with his fortune and felt compelled to use it for the greater good.

2. Pioneering "Giving While Living":

Chuck Feeney championed the concept of "giving while living." Instead of waiting to leave a bequest through a foundation after his death, he actively and intentionally gave away his wealth during his lifetime.

3. Anonymous Philanthropy:

Feeney's approach to philanthropy was marked by humility and a desire for anonymity. He believed that true giving should be devoid of personal recognition or gain.

For many years, he donated substantial sums of money anonymously, quietly making a difference in countless lives.

4. The Atlantic Philanthropies:

In 1982, Chuck Feeney established The Atlantic Philanthropies as the vehicle for his philanthropic efforts. This foundation supported a wide range of causes, with a focus on education, healthcare, social justice, human rights, and peace-building.

5. Diverse Philanthropic Initiatives:

Chuck Feeney's philanthropy encompassed a diverse array of initiatives. He funded scholarships, medical research, healthcare facilities, and efforts to promote social justice and human rights.

His donations also supported peace and reconciliation efforts in regions affected by conflict.

6. Fulfilling His Giving Pledge:

Chuck Feeney was an early signatory of the Giving Pledge, a commitment by billionaires to give away the majority of their wealth. He fulfilled this pledge by giving away his entire fortune.

7. Philanthropic Legacy:

Chuck Feeney's legacy is characterised by the profound impact his giving had on society. He actively sought to address systemic issues and create lasting change rather than simply providing temporary relief.

8. Closure of The Atlantic Philanthropies:

In 2020, Chuck Feeney achieved his goal of giving away his entire fortune. He officially closed The Atlantic Philanthropies, marking the culmination of his lifelong commitment to "giving while living."

Chuck Feeney's unwavering commitment to giving back has inspired countless individuals and philanthropists around the world. His approach to philanthropy, marked by humility, anonymity, and a deep desire to make a meaningful difference, challenges conventional notions of wealth and continues to shape the way philanthropy is practised today.

2.4:Challenges:

Chuck Feeney's philanthropic journey, marked by his commitment to "giving while living," was not without its challenges and obstacles. Over the years, he faced numerous hurdles in his quest to make a meaningful impact on society through his philanthropic efforts. Here are some of the challenges Chuck Feeney encountered:

1. Balancing Anonymity and Impact:

Chuck Feeney's commitment to anonymity posed a challenge. While he preferred to give anonymously to avoid personal recognition, this approach sometimes made it difficult to garner public support for the causes he championed.

2. Philanthropic Scale:

The scale of Chuck Feeney's philanthropy was vast, and managing the distribution of such substantial resources required careful planning and execution. Ensuring that funds were used effectively and efficiently was an ongoing challenge.

3. Diverse Philanthropic Initiatives:

Feeney's philanthropic efforts spanned a wide range of causes, from education and healthcare to social justice and peace-building. Coordinating and managing these diverse initiatives presented logistical and strategic challenges.

4. Complex Issues:

Many of the issues Chuck Feeney sought to address were complex and deeply rooted, such as social inequality and healthcare disparities. Effecting meaningful change in these areas required innovative solutions and sustained effort.

5. Advocacy and Awareness:

Chuck Feeney's preference for anonymity sometimes hindered the advocacy and awareness-raising efforts that are essential for addressing systemic issues. Advocacy can play a crucial role in driving change, and this challenge required creative strategies.

6. Legacy and Sustainability:

Chuck Feeney was committed to ensuring that the impact of his philanthropy would be sustainable long after his giving had ceased. This required careful planning and collaboration with grantees and partners.

7. Managing Expectations:

Chuck Feeney's extraordinary generosity set high expectations for the causes and organisations he supported. Balancing these expectations with the realities of philanthropic work was an ongoing challenge.

8. Navigating Geopolitical Complexities:

Supporting peace and reconciliation efforts in regions affected by conflict, such as Northern Ireland, involved navigating complex geopolitical dynamics. These challenges required diplomatic finesse.

9. Closing The Atlantic Philanthropies:

The process of closing The Atlantic Philanthropies, Chuck Feeney's foundation, was a monumental task. Ensuring that the remaining funds were distributed effectively and responsibly was a significant challenge.

Despite these challenges, Chuck Feeney remained steadfast in his commitment to making a positive impact on society. His ability to overcome obstacles, coupled with his humility and determination, allowed him to achieve his goal of giving away his entire fortune and leave a profound and lasting legacy in the world of philanthropy.

CHAPTER 3:The Quiet Philanthropist:

Chuck Feeney is often referred to as "The Quiet Philanthropist" due to his unique approach to giving and his commitment to anonymity. This nickname encapsulates his philanthropic journey, marked by a deliberate choice to remain in the background while making an extraordinary impact on the world.

1. The Anonymity Principle:

Chuck Feeney's philanthropic philosophy centred on anonymity. He believed that true giving should be devoid of personal recognition or gain. This principle guided his actions throughout his philanthropic career.

2. Shunning the Spotlight:

Unlike many high-profile philanthropists, Chuck Feeney actively avoided the limelight. He rarely sought public attention for his donations or philanthropic endeavours.

3. Anonymous Donations:

For many years, Feeney donated substantial sums of money anonymously. His gifts were often made through his foundation, The Atlantic Philanthropies, without attaching his name to them.

4. Motivation for Anonymity:

Chuck Feeney's motivation for remaining anonymous was rooted in his desire to focus on the causes he supported rather than on personal recognition. He believed that philanthropy should be about making a difference, not about the donor's ego.

5. Inspiring Others Quietly:

Feeney's quiet philanthropy served as an inspiration to others. His actions challenged conventional notions of giving and encouraged individuals and philanthropists to prioritise the impact of their donations over personal acclaim.

6. A Unique Legacy:

Chuck Feeney's unique approach to philanthropy left a distinctive legacy. His story became a symbol of humility, selflessness, and the power of giving without expecting recognition or praise.

7. Philanthropic Achievements Speak Louder:

Despite his preference for anonymity, Chuck Feeney's philanthropic achievements spoke louder than words. His commitment to "giving while living" and his substantial contributions to education, healthcare, social justice, and peace-building had a profound impact.

8. Fulfilment of The Giving Pledge:

As an early signatory of the Giving Pledge, Feeney exemplified the principles of the initiative by giving away his entire fortune while alive, demonstrating that philanthropy need not be about personal glory.

Chuck Feeney's legacy as "The Quiet Philanthropist" serves as a reminder that philanthropy is not defined by public recognition but by the positive change it creates. His humility and focus on making a meaningful impact on the world continue to inspire individuals and philanthropists to prioritise the greater good over personal acclaim.

3.1:Approach to Giving:

Chuck Feeney's approach to giving is characterised by a set of principles and values that distinguish his philanthropy as both unique and highly impactful. His approach, often described as "giving while living," has been a model for philanthropists around the world. Here are the key aspects of Chuck Feeney's approach to giving:

1. "Giving While Living":

Chuck Feeney's central philanthropic principle was the commitment to "giving while living." He believed in actively and intentionally donating his wealth during his lifetime to create a meaningful impact.

2. Anonymity and Humility:

Feeney shunned personal recognition and fame. He chose to remain anonymous for many years, directing his philanthropic efforts toward causes and organisations without attaching his name to the donations.

3. Impactful and Strategic Giving:

Feeney focused on achieving significant and strategic impact through his philanthropy. He sought to address root causes of societal issues and create lasting change rather than providing temporary relief.

4. Wide Range of Causes:

Chuck Feeney's philanthropic efforts encompassed a diverse array of causes, including education, healthcare, social justice, human rights, and peace-building. He recognized the interconnectedness of global challenges and addressed them comprehensively.

5. Hands-On Approach:

Feeney took a hands-on approach to philanthropy, actively engaging with the organisations and causes he supported. He sought to understand the issues at a deep level and collaborate closely with grantees.

6. Collaborative Partnerships:

Chuck Feeney valued collaboration and partnerships with other philanthropists, organisations, and governments. He believed in the power of collective efforts to effect change on a larger scale.

7. Results-Oriented Approach:

Feeney was results-oriented in his giving. He expected accountability and measurable outcomes from the organisations he supported, ensuring that his donations were used effectively.

8. Focus on Sustainability:

Sustainability was a key consideration in Feeney's philanthropy. He aimed to create lasting impact that would continue to benefit society long after his lifetime.

9. Fulfilment of the Giving Pledge:

Chuck Feeney was an early signatory of the Giving Pledge, committing to give away the majority of his wealth. He fulfilled this pledge by giving away his entire fortune, setting an example for other philanthropists.

10. Closing The Atlantic Philanthropies:

In 2020, Chuck Feeney closed The Atlantic Philanthropies, effectively ending his formal philanthropic operations. This marked the culmination of his commitment to "giving while living."

Chuck Feeney's approach to giving, marked by anonymity, humility, strategic impact, and a deep commitment to addressing global challenges, serves as an inspiration for philanthropists and individuals alike. His legacy reminds us that philanthropy is not about personal recognition but about making a meaningful difference in the world.

3.2:Fulfilment of the Giving Pledge:

Chuck Feeney's fulfilment of the Giving Pledge is a significant chapter in his philanthropic journey. The Giving Pledge is an initiative started by Warren Buffett and Bill and Melinda Gates, which encourages billionaires to commit to giving away the majority of their wealth during their lifetimes. Chuck Feeney's participation in and fulfilment of this pledge demonstrated his unwavering commitment to "giving while living."

1. Early Signatory of the Giving Pledge:
   Chuck Feeney was among the early signatories of the Giving Pledge when it was launched in 2010. His participation in this initiative signaled his dedication to directing his wealth toward philanthropy rather than personal accumulation.

2. Giving Away His Entire Fortune:
   Chuck Feeney's commitment to the Giving Pledge was not merely symbolic. He embarked on a mission to give

away his entire fortune, estimated to be in the billions of dollars, during his lifetime.

3. Quiet and Anonymity-Preserving Giving:

Feeney's approach to philanthropy remained consistent with his preference for anonymity. Much of his giving was done quietly and without public recognition, aligning with the core principles of the Giving Pledge.

4. Collaborative Philanthropy:

Chuck Feeney's participation in the Giving Pledge also exemplified his willingness to collaborate with other philanthropists. He recognized the collective impact that could be achieved by pooling resources and efforts. Chuck Feeney's fulfilment of the Giving Pledge is a significant chapter in his philanthropic journey. The Giving Pledge is an initiative started by Warren Buffett and Bill and Melinda Gates, which encourages billionaires to commit to giving away the majority of their wealth during their lifetimes. Chuck Feeney's participation in and fulfilment of this pledge demonstrated his unwavering commitment to "giving while living."

1. Early Signatory of the Giving Pledge:

Chuck Feeney was among the early signatories of the Giving Pledge when it was launched in 2010. His participation in this initiative signalled his dedication to directing his wealth toward philanthropy rather than personal accumulation.

2. Giving Away His Entire Fortune:

Chuck Feeney's commitment to the Giving Pledge was not merely symbolic. He embarked on a mission to give away his entire fortune, estimated to be in the billions of dollars, during his lifetime.

3. Quiet and Anonymity-Preserving Giving:

Feeney's approach to philanthropy remained consistent with his preference for anonymity. Much of his giving was done quietly and without public recognition, aligning with the core principles of the Giving Pledge.

4. Collaborative Philanthropy:

Chuck Feeney's participation in the Giving Pledge also exemplified his willingness to collaborate with other philanthropists. He recognized the collective impact that could be achieved by pooling resources and efforts.

5. Global Impact:

Fulfilling the Giving Pledge allowed Chuck Feeney to make a substantial global impact. His philanthropic endeavours touched various sectors, including education, healthcare, social justice, and peace-building.

6. Closing of The Atlantic Philanthropies:

In September 2020, Chuck Feeney achieved his goal of giving away his entire fortune. To mark this momentous occasion, he officially closed The Atlantic Philanthropies, the foundation through which much of his giving was administered.

7. A Pioneering Example:

Chuck Feeney's fulfilment of the Giving Pledge served as a pioneering example for other billionaires. His actions demonstrated that it was possible to give generously and strategically during one's lifetime, leaving a profound legacy of positive change.

8. Legacy of Impact:

Chuck Feeney's legacy is not defined by the wealth he accumulated but by the impact he created. His commitment to "giving while living" challenged conventional notions of philanthropy and inspired others to follow in his footsteps.

Chuck Feeney's fulfilment of the Giving Pledge is a testament to his belief in the power of philanthropy to make a positive difference in the world. His actions continue to inspire individuals and philanthropists to prioritise the greater good and actively use their wealth to address pressing societal issues.

7. A Pioneering Example:

Chuck Feeney's fulfilment of the Giving Pledge served as a pioneering example for other billionaires. His actions demonstrated that it was possible to give generously and strategically during one's lifetime, leaving a profound legacy of positive change.

8. Legacy of Impact:

Chuck Feeney's legacy is not defined by the wealth he accumulated but by the impact he created. His commitment to "giving while living" challenged conventional notions of philanthropy and inspired others to follow in his footsteps.

Chuck Feeney's fulfilment of the Giving Pledge is a testament to his belief in the power of philanthropy to make a positive difference in the world. His actions continue to inspire individuals and philanthropists to prioritise the greater good and actively use their wealth to address pressing societal issues.

3.3:A Pioneering Example:

Chuck Feeney's philanthropic journey serves as a pioneering example of how one individual's commitment to "giving while living" can create a profound and lasting impact on the world. His approach to philanthropy, marked by humility, strategic giving, and a relentless dedication to making a difference, has inspired countless individuals and philanthropists to follow in his footsteps. Here are the key aspects of Chuck Feeney's pioneering example:

1. Commitment to "Giving While Living":
Chuck Feeney's unwavering commitment to giving away his entire fortune during his lifetime challenged conventional notions of philanthropy. He believed that wealth should be used to address pressing societal issues in real-time.

2. Anonymity and Humility:
Feeney's preference for anonymity and humility in giving set him apart. He actively avoided public recognition and personal gain, focusing solely on the causes and organisations he supported.

3. Global Philanthropic Reach:

Chuck Feeney's philanthropy had a global reach, touching a wide range of causes and initiatives. He addressed issues spanning education, healthcare, social justice, human rights, and peace-building on an international scale.

4. Strategic Impact:

Feeney was known for his strategic approach to philanthropy. He sought to address root causes and create lasting change rather than simply providing temporary relief. His philanthropic investments were carefully planned for maximum impact.

5. Collaborative Philanthropy:

Chuck Feeney valued collaboration and partnerships with other philanthropists, organisations, and governments. He believed in the power of collective efforts to effect change on a larger scale.

6. The Giving Pledge Pioneer:

As an early signatory of the Giving Pledge, Feeney served as a pioneering example for other billionaires. He demonstrated that it was possible to actively and intentionally give away one's wealth to benefit society.

7. Closure of The Atlantic Philanthropies:

In 2020, Chuck Feeney achieved his goal of giving away his entire fortune and officially closed The Atlantic Philanthropies, the foundation through which he channelled his giving.

8. Inspiring Future Generations:

Chuck Feeney's philanthropic journey continues to inspire individuals, philanthropists, and organisations to embrace his values of selflessness and impact-driven giving.

9. A Legacy of Giving:

Chuck Feeney's legacy is not one of personal wealth or recognition but of selfless giving and the transformative power of philanthropy. His example encourages others to consider how they can use their resources to make the world a better place.

Chuck Feeney's pioneering example challenges individuals to think beyond personal gain and leave a legacy of positive change. His life's work demonstrates that philanthropy can be a force for good when guided by a deep sense of responsibility and a commitment to making a difference in the world.

3.4:The Beginnings of The Atlantic Philanthropies:

The beginnings of The Atlantic Philanthropies marked a pivotal moment in Chuck Feeney's philanthropic journey. This foundation served as the primary vehicle through which he directed his substantial wealth toward a wide range of charitable causes. The story of The Atlantic Philanthropies underscores Feeney's commitment to "giving while living" and his desire to create a meaningful and lasting impact on society. Here are the key aspects of the foundation's early days:

1. Foundation Establishment:

The Atlantic Philanthropies was officially established by Chuck Feeney in 1982. It was created as a vehicle to channel his philanthropic efforts and fulfil his commitment to giving away his wealth during his lifetime.

2. Core Values and Vision:

From its inception, The Atlantic Philanthropies was guided by a set of core values, including humility, anonymity, and a focus on creating sustainable change. Feeney's vision was to address pressing societal issues through strategic and impactful giving.

3. Diverse Philanthropic Initiatives:

The foundation's early years saw a diverse array of philanthropic initiatives. Chuck Feeney's commitment to addressing various sectors, including education, healthcare, social justice, human rights, and peace-building, began to take shape.

4. Anonymity-Preserving Giving:

One of the foundation's defining features was its commitment to anonymity-preserving giving. Much of Chuck Feeney's donations were made quietly, without attaching his name to them. This approach was consistent with his preference for humility.

5. Collaboration and Partnerships:

The Atlantic Philanthropies actively sought collaboration and partnerships with other philanthropists, organisations, and governments. This collaborative approach allowed for greater collective impact.

6. Emphasis on Accountability and Impact:

The foundation emphasised accountability and impact assessment. Grants were made to organisations and initiatives that demonstrated a clear commitment to achieving measurable outcomes and long-term change.

7. A Global Reach:

The Atlantic Philanthropies had a global reach, funding projects and initiatives in multiple countries. Feeney's belief in addressing international challenges on a global scale became a hallmark of the foundation's work.

8. A Growing Endowment:

While Chuck Feeney directed the majority of his wealth to philanthropy, The Atlantic Philanthropies also managed its endowment and investments to ensure its sustainability and ability to continue making an impact.

The beginnings of The Atlantic Philanthropies marked the formalisation of Chuck Feeney's lifelong commitment to philanthropy. Through the foundation, he channelled his resources, values, and vision into creating positive change in various sectors and regions around the world. The foundation's early years laid the groundwork for decades of impactful giving and a profound legacy of selfless generosity.

CHAPTER 4:Visionary Giving:

Chuck Feeney's approach to philanthropy can be described as visionary giving. His remarkable journey as a philanthropist was marked by a forward-thinking and innovative approach to making a meaningful impact on the world. Here are the key elements that define Chuck Feeney's visionary giving:

1. "Giving While Living":

Chuck Feeney's commitment to "giving while living" exemplifies his visionary approach. He believed that philanthropy should be an immediate response to societal challenges, rather than a deferred action for the future.

2. Immediate and Tangible Impact:

Visionary giving, in Feeney's view, was about creating immediate and tangible impact. He prioritised addressing pressing issues during his lifetime to effect positive change as quickly as possible.

3. Strategic and Thoughtful Investments:

Feeney's visionary giving was characterized by strategic thinking. He carefully selected causes and organisations that aligned with his values and had the potential for significant and long-lasting change.

4. Anonymity-Preserving Approach:

Maintaining anonymity was a core principle of Chuck Feeney's giving. He believed that the focus should always be on the causes and the people they served, not on the donor. This approach allowed his philanthropy to speak for itself.

5. Global Perspective:

Visionary giving necessitates a global perspective, and Chuck Feeney's philanthropy had a worldwide reach. He recognized that many societal challenges were not confined by borders and worked to address them on an international scale.

6. Collaboration and Partnerships:

Chuck Feeney's visionary giving included a willingness to collaborate and partner with others. He understood that collective efforts could amplify the impact of philanthropic endeavors and tackle complex issues more effectively.

7. Transparency and Accountability:
Visionary giving requires transparency and accountability. Feeney emphasised the importance of measuring impact and holding organisations accountable for the outcomes of their work.

8. Fulfilment of the Giving Pledge:
- As one of the early signatories of the Giving Pledge, Feeney demonstrated the visionary idea that significant wealth should be used for the betterment of society. He fulfilled this pledge by giving away his entire fortune during his lifetime.

9. A Legacy of Inspiration:
Chuck Feeney's visionary giving continues to inspire others. His legacy challenges individuals and

philanthropists to consider how they can use their resources to address pressing global challenges and create a better future.

Chuck Feeney's visionary giving serves as a model for how philanthropy can be a proactive force for positive change. His approach, guided by a deep sense of responsibility and a commitment to immediate impact, reminds us that philanthropy has the potential to shape a better world for current and future generations.

4.1:Funding Higher Education:

Chuck Feeney's philanthropic legacy includes significant contributions to higher education, reflecting his belief in the transformative power of education. Feeney's funding of higher education institutions and programs aimed to provide opportunities for individuals to access quality education and pursue their dreams. Here's an overview of his contributions to higher education:

1. Cornell University:

Chuck Feeney made substantial contributions to his alma mater, Cornell University. He supported various initiatives, including scholarships and the construction of facilities, to enhance the educational experience for students.

2. University of California, San Francisco (UCSF):

Feeney's generosity extended to the University of California, San Francisco. His donations helped fund the construction of a state-of-the-art biomedical research building, contributing to advancements in medical science.

3. Atlantic Philanthropies' Investment in Higher Education:

Through The Atlantic Philanthropies, Feeney supported higher education institutions in several countries. His funding went toward scholarships, research programs, and infrastructure improvements, benefiting students and faculty.

4. Trinity College Dublin:

Feeney's contributions to Trinity College Dublin in Ireland had a profound impact. His support included funding for research, scholarships, and initiatives aimed at advancing education and fostering innovation.

5. Technological University Dublin:

Chuck Feeney's philanthropy extended to Technological University Dublin, where his donations funded projects such as student scholarships and advancements in technology and innovation.

6. Commitment to Accessible Education:

Feeney's commitment to accessible education was evident in his focus on scholarships and financial aid programs. He aimed to reduce financial barriers and enable students from diverse backgrounds to pursue higher education.

7. Research and Innovation:

In addition to scholarships, Feeney's funding supported research and innovation in various fields. His contributions facilitated groundbreaking discoveries and advancements in science and technology.

8. Creating Opportunities:

Chuck Feeney's investments in higher education created opportunities for countless individuals to pursue their academic and career goals. His philanthropic efforts aimed to empower students to reach their full potential.

9. A Lasting Educational Legacy:

Feeney's support for higher education institutions left a lasting legacy. His vision of education as a means to drive positive change and improve society continues to impact students, researchers, and educators.

Chuck Feeney's commitment to funding higher education reflects his belief that knowledge and education are powerful tools for personal growth and societal progress. His philanthropic contributions have opened doors for countless individuals to access quality education and contribute to the betterment of their communities and the world.

4.2:Medical Research:

Chuck Feeney's philanthropy extended to the realm of medical research, where he made significant contributions aimed at advancing scientific knowledge, improving healthcare, and finding innovative solutions to pressing medical challenges. Here's an overview of Chuck Feeney's impact on medical research:

1. University of California, San Francisco (UCSF):
   Chuck Feeney's philanthropic support for UCSF included funding for biomedical research. His contributions played a crucial role in advancing medical science and the development of cutting-edge treatments and therapies.

2. Biomedical Research Initiatives:
   Through The Atlantic Philanthropies, Feeney supported various biomedical research initiatives, focusing on areas such as cancer research,

neurodegenerative diseases, and infectious diseases. His funding enabled scientists and researchers to make significant breakthroughs.

3. Advancements in Healthcare Technology:

Feeney's contributions also supported the development and implementation of healthcare technology and innovative medical devices. His funding helped improve patient care and medical practices.

4. Clinical Trials and Drug Development:

Chuck Feeney's philanthropy facilitated clinical trials and drug development programs. His support was instrumental in bringing new medications and treatments to patients, particularly those with life-threatening conditions.

5. Medical Education and Training:

Feeney recognized the importance of medical education and training. His funding supported medical schools and training programs, ensuring that future healthcare professionals receive high-quality education.

6. Global Health Initiatives:

Feeney's commitment to medical research extended to global health initiatives. He supported efforts to combat infectious diseases, improve healthcare infrastructure in underserved regions, and enhance access to healthcare services worldwide.

7. Accelerating Scientific Discovery:

Chuck Feeney's philanthropy had a direct impact on accelerating scientific discovery in various medical fields. His investments in research projects and institutions contributed to advancements that have saved lives and improved public health.

8. Collaborative Research:

Feeney believed in the power of collaborative research. His funding often encouraged partnerships between research institutions, healthcare organisations, and scientists, fostering a collaborative approach to solving complex medical challenges.

9. Legacy of Medical Progress:

Chuck Feeney's contributions to medical research left a lasting legacy of progress. His philanthropic endeavours continue to benefit patients, researchers, and healthcare professionals, contributing to the ongoing improvement of healthcare worldwide.

Chuck Feeney's commitment to medical research exemplifies his belief in the potential for science and innovation to address some of the world's most pressing health issues. His philanthropy has played a pivotal role in advancing medical knowledge, improving patient care, and ultimately saving lives.

4.3:Advancing Social Justice:

Chuck Feeney's commitment to advancing social justice was a central pillar of his philanthropic work. Throughout his life, he dedicated substantial resources and effort to promote equality, human rights, and social equity. Here's an overview of Chuck Feeney's impact on advancing social justice:

1. Civil Rights and Racial Equality:

Feeney's philanthropy supported civil rights organisations and initiatives aimed at addressing racial inequality. His funding contributed to efforts to combat discrimination, promote racial justice, and create opportunities for marginalized communities.

2. Criminal Justice Reform:

Chuck Feeney's commitment to social justice extended to criminal justice reform. He supported organisations working to reform the criminal justice system, advocate for fair sentencing, and address issues of mass incarceration.

3. Human Rights Advocacy:

Feeney's philanthropy included support for human rights organisations around the world. He championed causes related to freedom, democracy, and the protection of human rights, particularly in regions facing political turmoil and oppression.

4. LGBTQ+ Rights:

Feeney's contributions also extended to LGBTQ+ rights organisations. His funding helped advance LGBTQ+ equality and inclusion, contributing to the broader movement for equal rights and acceptance.

5. Advocacy for Marginalised Communities:

Feeney's philanthropic efforts focused on marginalised communities, including refugees, immigrants, and Indigenous peoples. His funding supported initiatives aimed at improving the living conditions and rights of these populations.

6. Social Equity and Economic Opportunity:

Feeney believed in providing economic opportunities to those who had been historically marginalised. His funding supported programs and initiatives aimed at reducing economic disparities and promoting social equity.

7. Education as a Catalyst:

Education was a key tool in Feeney's approach to social justice. He funded educational programs that aimed to uplift disadvantaged individuals and communities, providing them with the skills and knowledge to improve their lives.

8. Conflict Resolution and Peace-Building:

Feeney's philanthropy extended to peace-building efforts in conflict regions. He supported organisations and initiatives focused on conflict resolution, reconciliation, and promoting peaceful coexistence.

9. Advocating for Systemic Change:

Chuck Feeney's commitment to social justice was not just about addressing immediate issues but advocating for systemic change. His funding often targeted root causes of injustice to create lasting impact.

10. Inspiring Others:

Feeney's philanthropic efforts in the realm of social justice continue to inspire individuals, organisations, and philanthropists to engage in meaningful advocacy and activism to advance social equality and justice.

Chuck Feeney's legacy in advancing social justice demonstrates the potential for philanthropy to drive meaningful change in society. His dedication to addressing systemic issues, advocating for marginalised communities, and promoting human rights serves as an enduring example of how individuals can use their resources to create a more just and equitable world.Chuck Feeney's life and philanthropic journey continue to serve as a profound source of inspiration for individuals, philanthropists, and organisations worldwide. His unwavering commitment to "giving while living," humility, and dedication to making a positive impact on society has left an indelible mark on those who have followed his story. Here's how Chuck Feeney continues to inspire others:

1. Selflessness and Humility:

Chuck Feeney's commitment to anonymity and humility in giving has inspired others to prioritise the greater good over personal recognition. His example highlights the power of selfless philanthropy.

2. Strategic and Impact-Driven Giving:

Feeney's strategic approach to philanthropy, focusing on creating lasting impact and addressing root causes, encourages others to think critically about their own giving and its potential for positive change.

3. "Giving While Living" Philosophy:

Feeney's philosophy of "giving while living" challenges the traditional approach to philanthropy and inspires individuals to actively use their resources to address pressing societal issues during their lifetimes.

4. Global Perspective:

His global philanthropy demonstrates the importance of addressing international challenges and inspires individuals to think beyond borders when considering ways to make a difference.

5. Collaborative Philanthropy:

Feeney's willingness to collaborate with other philanthropists, organisations, and governments underscores the power of collective efforts to tackle complex issues and amplify impact.

6. Fulfilment of the Giving Pledge:

As an early signatory of the Giving Pledge, Chuck Feeney's commitment to giving away the majority of his wealth encourages other billionaires to consider how they can contribute to the betterment of society.

7. Embracing Anonymity:

Feeney's preference for anonymity in his giving showcases that philanthropy doesn't need personal recognition to be impactful. This inspires donors to give for the sake of the causes they support, not for personal gain.

8. Closing of The Atlantic Philanthropies:

The closure of The Atlantic Philanthropies, marking the fulfilment of Feeney's philanthropic mission, serves as a powerful example of setting and achieving audacious goals.

9. Leaving a Legacy of Positive Change:

Chuck Feeney's legacy is defined by the profound and lasting impact he created through his philanthropy. His example encourages individuals to consider how they can leave a legacy that benefits society.

10. A Vision for a Better World:

Feeney's life story embodies the vision of a world where individuals use their resources to address societal challenges and create a more equitable and just society.

Chuck Feeney's enduring legacy is a testament to the transformative power of philanthropy when guided by a deep sense of responsibility and a commitment to the well-being of others. His life's work continues to inspire and challenge individuals to be agents of positive change in the world.

4.4:Human Rights:

Chuck Feeney's philanthropic endeavours extended to the realm of human rights, reflecting his unwavering commitment to promoting and protecting the fundamental rights and dignity of individuals around the world. Here's an overview of Chuck Feeney's impact on advancing human rights:

1. Supporting Human Rights Organizations:

Chuck Feeney's philanthropy included generous support for human rights organisations globally. He recognized the critical role these organisations played in advocating for and defending the rights of individuals, particularly in regions facing political turmoil and oppression.

2. Freedom and Democracy Promotion:

Feeney's contributions supported initiatives aimed at promoting freedom, democracy, and good governance.

His funding empowered organisations that worked to strengthen democratic institutions, protect civil liberties, and ensure the rule of law.

3. Protecting Vulnerable Populations:

Feeney's philanthropy focused on protecting vulnerable and marginalised populations, including refugees, immigrants, and Indigenous peoples. His support aimed to improve the living conditions and rights of these communities, particularly in regions facing displacement and discrimination.

4. LGBTQ+ Rights Advocacy:

Chuck Feeney's contributions also extended to LGBTQ+ rights organisations. He actively supported initiatives that sought to advance LGBTQ+ equality, end discrimination, and promote acceptance and inclusion.

5. Humanitarian Efforts in Conflict Zones:

Feeney's commitment to human rights included funding humanitarian efforts in conflict zones. His philanthropy provided aid and relief to individuals and communities affected by armed conflicts, contributing to the protection of human rights in these challenging environments.

6. Advocacy Against Torture and Injustice:

Feeney's support for organizations combating torture and injustice underscored his commitment to preventing human rights abuses. His contributions contributed to raising awareness and advocating for the humane treatment of all individuals.

7. Legal Aid and Access to Justice:

Feeney recognized the importance of legal aid and access to justice for marginalised populations. His funding supported initiatives that provided legal assistance to those in need, ensuring their rights were upheld.

8. Advancing Gender Equality:

Feeney's philanthropy also extended to advancing gender equality and women's rights. He supported organisations and programs that promoted gender equity and women's empowerment.

9. A Voice for the Voiceless:

Chuck Feeney's contributions gave a voice to those who often went unheard. His dedication to human rights inspired others to stand up for justice, even in the face of adversity.

10. Leaving a Legacy of Human Dignity:

Feeney's legacy is one that champions human dignity and the importance of protecting the rights and freedoms of all individuals. His philanthropic work continues to inspire efforts to create a more just and equitable world.

Chuck Feeney's commitment to human rights demonstrates the profound impact philanthropy can have in safeguarding the rights and dignity of individuals. His legacy challenges individuals and organisations to actively work toward a world where human rights are universally respected and protected.

4.5:Global Impact of His Philanthropy:

The global impact of Chuck Feeney's philanthropy is nothing short of extraordinary. His unwavering commitment to "giving while living" and his visionary approach to philanthropy have left an indelible mark on numerous causes, institutions, and communities around the world. Here's a closer look at the global impact of Chuck Feeney's philanthropy:

1. Education and Research:

Feeney's investments in education and research spanned the globe. He supported universities, schools, and research institutions in the United States, Ireland, Australia, and beyond. His funding has empowered countless individuals to access quality education and pursue groundbreaking research.

2. Healthcare and Medical Research:

Chuck Feeney's contributions to healthcare and medical research extended to various countries. His support for hospitals, medical schools, and research centres has advanced healthcare systems and facilitated groundbreaking medical discoveries worldwide.

3. Peace and Conflict Resolution:

Feeney's philanthropy played a role in peace-building efforts in regions affected by conflict. His funding supported initiatives aimed at reconciliation, conflict resolution, and the promotion of peace in countries facing long-standing disputes.

4. Social Justice and Human Rights:

His commitment to social justice and human rights had a global reach. Feeney's contributions supported organisations and initiatives working to combat discrimination, protect civil liberties, and promote human rights on an international scale.

5. Economic Development:

Feeney's funding of economic development programs had an impact in multiple countries, particularly in regions with economic challenges. His contributions aimed to create economic opportunities and alleviate poverty.

6. Philanthropic Collaboration:

Chuck Feeney's collaborative approach to philanthropy encouraged partnerships and cooperation among philanthropists, governments, and organisations globally. This approach fostered collective efforts to address complex global challenges.

7. Global Philanthropic Influence:

As a signatory of the Giving Pledge, Feeney's commitment to giving away the majority of his wealth during his lifetime inspired other billionaires to consider how their resources could make a difference on a global scale.

8. Inspiring Future Generations:

Feeney's life and philanthropic journey serve as a source of inspiration for individuals and future philanthropists worldwide. His example challenges others to use their resources for the betterment of society and the world.

9. Closing of The Atlantic Philanthropies:

The closure of The Atlantic Philanthropies marked the culmination of Chuck Feeney's philanthropic mission. This act demonstrated his commitment to his vision and the impact he aimed to achieve.

Chuck Feeney's global impact is a testament to the transformative power of philanthropy when guided by a deep sense of responsibility, humility, and a vision for a better world. His philanthropic legacy continues to inspire individuals and organisations to address pressing global challenges and create lasting positive change.

CHAPTER 5:The Art of Giving While Living:

Chuck Feeney's philanthropic philosophy, often referred to as "giving while living," is a testament to the art of making a meaningful impact on the world during one's lifetime. This approach, which distinguished Feeney's philanthropy, is characterised by several key principles and strategies:

1. A Commitment to Immediate Impact:

Chuck Feeney believed in the urgency of addressing societal issues and saw philanthropy as a way to create immediate and tangible change. Rather than accumulating wealth for the future, he sought to address pressing needs in the present.

2. Humility and Anonymity:

Feeney's preference for anonymity was integral to his philosophy. He actively avoided personal recognition and sought to keep the focus on the causes and organisations he supported. This humility allowed his philanthropy to speak louder than his name.

3. Strategic Giving:

Giving while living involves strategic philanthropy. Chuck Feeney carefully selected causes and organisations that aligned with his values and had the potential for significant and lasting impact. His philanthropic investments were driven by a desire for meaningful outcomes.

4. A Global Perspective:

Feeney's philanthropy had a global reach. He recognized that many challenges transcended borders and that a global perspective was essential for addressing issues like education, healthcare, social justice, and peace-building effectively.

5. Collaborative Partnerships:

Chuck Feeney valued collaboration and partnerships with other philanthropists, governments, and organisations. He believed that working together could amplify the impact of philanthropic efforts and address complex challenges more effectively.

6. Measuring Impact and Accountability:

The art of giving while living involves rigorous accountability and impact assessment. Feeney expected the organisations he supported to demonstrate measurable progress and results.

7. Fulfilment of the Giving Pledge:

As an early signatory of the Giving Pledge, Chuck Feeney fulfilled his commitment to give away the majority of his wealth during his lifetime. This pledge further underscored his philosophy of active and intentional giving.

8. Closing The Atlantic Philanthropies:

The art of giving while living reached its pinnacle when Chuck Feeney officially closed The Atlantic Philanthropies in 2020. This marked the fulfilment of his goal to give away his entire fortune while alive.

9. A Legacy of Impact:

Chuck Feeney's art of giving while living serves as a model for philanthropists and individuals alike. His legacy is not defined by the wealth he accumulated but by the profound and lasting impact he created through his selfless and strategic giving.

Chuck Feeney's philanthropic approach demonstrates that generosity, humility, and a commitment to immediate impact can be powerful tools for creating positive change in the world. His art of giving while living continues to inspire others to prioritise meaningful philanthropy and work towards addressing pressing societal challenges during their lifetimes.Chuck Feeney's legacy is undeniably one of profound and lasting impact. His extraordinary philanthropic journey, guided by the principles of "giving while living," humility, and strategic giving, has left an indelible mark on the world. Here are key aspects of Chuck Feeney's legacy of impact:

1. Transformational Giving:

Chuck Feeney's philanthropy was transformational in nature. His generous donations and strategic investments had a significant and positive impact on a wide range of causes, including education, healthcare, social justice, human rights, and peace-building.

2. Creating Lasting Change:

Feeney's focus on addressing root causes and creating lasting change set his philanthropy apart. He sought to tackle systemic issues and contribute to solutions that would endure long after his lifetime.

3. Global Reach:

The legacy of Chuck Feeney's impact extended globally. His philanthropic efforts touched the lives of countless individuals in numerous countries, emphasising his commitment to addressing international challenges on a global scale.

4. Anonymity-Preserving Giving:

A hallmark of Feeney's legacy was his commitment to anonymity. He gave quietly and avoided personal recognition, ensuring that the spotlight remained on the causes he supported rather than on himself.

5. Inspiring Future Generations:

Chuck Feeney's life and philanthropy continue to inspire individuals, philanthropists, and organisations. His legacy challenges others to prioritise the greater good and actively use their resources to make a difference in the world.

6. The Fulfilment of The Giving Pledge:

As an early signatory of the Giving Pledge, Chuck Feeney fulfilled his commitment to give away the majority of his wealth during his lifetime. This action served as a pioneering example for other billionaires, demonstrating the impact of "giving while living."

7. Closing The Atlantic Philanthropies:

Chuck Feeney achieved his goal of giving away his entire fortune and officially closed The Atlantic Philanthropies in 2020. This marked the culmination of his commitment to philanthropy and his legacy of selfless giving.

8. Philanthropy That Speaks Louder:

Feeney's legacy challenges the notion that philanthropy is solely about personal recognition. Instead, his life's work demonstrates that true impact comes from selflessness, humility, and a relentless commitment to making the world a better place.

9. A Visionary Legacy:

Chuck Feeney's legacy is visionary in that it calls on individuals and philanthropists to think beyond personal gain and to consider how they can contribute to positive change during their lifetimes.

Chuck Feeney's legacy of impact serves as a testament to the transformative power of philanthropy when guided by a deep sense of responsibility and a commitment to the greater good. His life's work continues to inspire individuals and philanthropists to embrace his values and leave a legacy of positive change in the world.

5.1:The Decision to Give Away His Wealth During His Lifetime:

One of the defining aspects of Chuck Feeney's philanthropic journey was his unwavering decision to give away his entire wealth during his lifetime. This commitment, known as "giving while living," set him apart as a visionary philanthropist and had a profound impact on the world. Here's an exploration of Chuck Feeney's decision to give away his wealth:

1. Embracing the Philosophy:

Chuck Feeney wholeheartedly embraced the philosophy of "giving while living." He believed that philanthropy should be an active response to pressing societal issues, rather than a deferred action for the future.

2. Creating Immediate Impact:

Feeney's decision was driven by a desire to create immediate and tangible impact. He wanted to see the results of his philanthropy during his lifetime and witness the positive changes it brought about.

3. Challenging Traditional Philanthropy:

By choosing to give away his wealth while he was alive, Feeney challenged the traditional approach to philanthropy, which often involved creating foundations with an indefinite lifespan. His decision encouraged other philanthropists to consider more proactive giving.

4. Anonymity and Humility:

Feeney's commitment to anonymity and humility was closely linked to his decision. He gave quietly, without seeking personal recognition, allowing his philanthropy to speak for itself.

5. A Sense of Urgency:

Feeney's sense of urgency was evident in his decision. He believed that many of the world's challenges required immediate attention and that philanthropy could be a powerful force for change.

6. Pioneering the Giving Pledge:

As one of the early signatories of the Giving Pledge, Feeney inspired other billionaires to commit to giving away the majority of their wealth during their lifetimes. His decision influenced a new generation of philanthropists.

7. Fulfilling a Vision:

Chuck Feeney's decision to give while living was integral to fulfilling his vision of creating a better world. He actively worked to achieve this vision through strategic giving.

8. A Legacy of Impact:

Feeney's decision resulted in a legacy of impact that will endure for generations. His philanthropy has left a profound mark on education, healthcare, social justice, and numerous other areas.

9. Closing of The Atlantic Philanthropies:

The closure of The Atlantic Philanthropies in 2020 marked the culmination of Chuck Feeney's mission to give away his entire fortune. It exemplified his commitment to the principles of "giving while living."

10. Inspiring Others:

Perhaps most importantly, Chuck Feeney's decision to give away his wealth during his lifetime continues to inspire individuals, philanthropists, and organisations to consider how they can make a meaningful impact on the world in their lifetimes.

Chuck Feeney's decision to "give while living" serves as a beacon of inspiration for those who believe in the power of philanthropy to effect positive change. His visionary approach challenges the notion that wealth must be hoarded or preserved for the future, showing that it can be a dynamic force for good when used to address the world's most pressing challenges today.

5.2:Fulfilling a Vision:

Fulfilling a vision was at the heart of Chuck Feeney's philanthropic journey. His decision to give away his entire wealth during his lifetime was driven by a deeply held vision of creating a better world, one marked by equity, justice, and positive transformation. Here's a closer look at how Chuck Feeney fulfilled his vision through philanthropy:

1. Defining a Clear Vision:
   Chuck Feeney's philanthropic journey began with a clear and ambitious vision. He envisioned a world where resources were used to address pressing social issues, promote education, advance healthcare, and champion human rights.

2. "Giving While Living" Philosophy:
   Feeney's vision was closely aligned with the philosophy of "giving while living." He believed that philanthropy should be proactive, addressing immediate

challenges, rather than deferring action to future generations.

3. Strategic and Impactful Giving:

To fulfil his vision, Feeney adopted a strategic approach to philanthropy. He meticulously identified causes and organisations that aligned with his vision and had the potential for significant, lasting impact.

4. Education as a Catalyst:

A cornerstone of Feeney's vision was the belief in education as a catalyst for societal change. He saw education as a means to empower individuals and communities to shape their own destinies.

5. Global Reach:

Feeney's vision extended beyond national borders. He recognized that many global challenges required international collaboration and resources, leading to his philanthropic efforts spanning multiple countries.

6. Encouraging Collaborative Philanthropy:

Chuck Feeney's vision included encouraging collaboration among philanthropists, governments, and organisations. He believed that collective efforts could amplify impact and address complex issues more effectively.

7. Anonymity Preserving His Vision:

Feeney's commitment to anonymity was a deliberate choice to preserve the focus on his vision rather than himself. He believed that the causes he supported should take centre stage.

8. Empowering Others:

Part of Feeney's vision was to inspire others to take action. He wanted his philanthropy to serve as a model and catalyst for individuals and organisations to contribute to positive societal change.

9. The Closing of The Atlantic Philanthropies:

The closure of The Atlantic Philanthropies in 2020 marked the fulfilment of Chuck Feeney's vision. It was the culmination of his mission to give away his wealth to create a lasting legacy of impact.

10. A Legacy of Transformation:

Chuck Feeney's philanthropic legacy is a testament to the fulfilment of his vision. His contributions have transformed education, healthcare, social justice, and many other areas, leaving a lasting imprint on the world.

Chuck Feeney's commitment to fulfilling his vision through philanthropy serves as a remarkable example of how one individual's dedication, resourcefulness, and visionary thinking can bring about profound and positive change in the world. His legacy continues to inspire others to envision a better future and work tirelessly to make that vision a reality.

5.3:Philanthropic Principles:

Chuck Feeney's philanthropic journey was guided by a set of core principles that reflected his values, vision, and approach to making a positive impact on the world. These philanthropic principles not only shaped his giving but also continue to inspire individuals and organisations globally. Here are Chuck Feeney's key philanthropic principles:

1. "Giving While Living":
   At the heart of Feeney's philanthropy was the principle of "giving while living." He believed in actively using his wealth to address pressing societal issues during his lifetime, rather than waiting for future generations to distribute his fortune.

2. Anonymity and Humility:
   Feeney was known for his commitment to anonymity and humility in giving. He preferred to remain behind the scenes, allowing his philanthropy to speak for itself and avoiding personal recognition.

3. High Impact and Effectiveness:
   Feeney's philanthropy was marked by a relentless focus on high impact. He sought out opportunities and

causes where his contributions could make a significant and lasting difference.

4. Strategic Giving:

Chuck Feeney's giving was strategic and calculated. He carefully selected causes and organisations that aligned with his vision and were well-positioned to bring about meaningful change.

5. Collaboration and Partnerships:

Feeney recognized the importance of collaboration in philanthropy. He actively sought partnerships with other philanthropists, governments, and organisations to amplify the impact of his giving.

6. Global Perspective:

His philanthropy was not limited by geographical boundaries. Feeney believed in addressing global challenges and supported initiatives in multiple countries to create a broader impact.

7. Tackling Root Causes:

Feeney's approach was focused on addressing root causes of societal issues rather than merely addressing symptoms. He aimed to create systemic change and sustainable solutions.

8. Urgency and Timeliness:

Feeney had a sense of urgency in his giving. He believed that many challenges required immediate attention and action, and he acted swiftly to address them.

9. Legacy through Impact:

Rather than seeking personal legacy or recognition, Chuck Feeney aimed to leave a legacy of impact. He wanted his philanthropy to be remembered for the positive change it brought about.

10. Encouraging Others:

Feeney's philanthropic principles included inspiring others to take action. He hoped that his journey would motivate individuals and organisations to engage in meaningful philanthropy and contribute to a better world.

11. The Fulfilment of Pledges:

Chuck Feeney honoured his commitments and pledges, including being one of the earliest signatories of the Giving Pledge—a commitment by billionaires to give away the majority of their wealth to address society's most pressing issues.

Chuck Feeney's philanthropic principles are a testament to his profound dedication to making the world a better place. His legacy continues to inspire individuals and philanthropists to adopt similar principles, emphasising the importance of humility, impact-driven giving, and proactive efforts to address global challenges.

5.4:Strategies:

Chuck Feeney's philanthropic strategies were characterised by a thoughtful and deliberate approach aimed at maximising the impact of his giving. Over the years, he developed and refined strategies that allowed him to effectively address a wide range of societal issues. Here are some of the key philanthropic strategies employed by Chuck Feeney:

1. Focus on High-Impact Areas:

Feeney's philanthropic efforts were concentrated on areas where he believed he could make a significant difference. This included education, healthcare, social justice, and scientific research.

2. Direct Giving:

Feeney preferred direct giving to ensure that the majority of his funds reached the intended beneficiaries. He often bypassed intermediaries to minimise administrative costs and maximise the impact of his donations.

3. Long-Term Commitment:

Chuck Feeney's philanthropy was marked by long-term commitments. He often provided multi-year grants and support, allowing organisations to plan and implement sustainable initiatives.

4. Strategic Partnerships:

Collaboration was a cornerstone of Feeney's strategy. He actively sought partnerships with other philanthropists, governments, and organisations to pool resources and expertise for greater impact.

5. Anonymity and Humility:

Feeney's commitment to anonymity and humility allowed him to prioritise the causes he supported over personal recognition. This approach kept the focus on the issues rather than the donor.

6. Leveraging Challenge Grants:

He utilised challenge grants effectively, encouraging other donors to match his contributions. This strategy not only multiplied the impact of his giving but also inspired additional support.

7. Rigorous Evaluation:

Feeney employed rigorous evaluation processes to assess the effectiveness of his philanthropic investments. He regularly reviewed the outcomes of his donations to ensure they aligned with his goals.

8. Capacity Building:

His philanthropy often included support for capacity-building initiatives within organisations. This approach strengthened the capabilities of nonprofits to fulfil their missions more effectively.

9. Global Reach:

Chuck Feeney's philanthropic footprint extended globally. He recognized that many of the world's challenges required international solutions, leading to his support of initiatives in various countries.

10. Philanthropic Exit Strategy:

Feeney had a well-defined exit strategy for his philanthropy. He set a specific timeline for completing his giving and followed through with the closure of The Atlantic Philanthropies once his mission was fulfilled.

11. Encouraging Transparency:

While Feeney himself maintained anonymity, he encouraged transparency in philanthropy overall. He believed that transparency could lead to greater accountability and impact across the sector.

12. Fulfilling Commitments:

Chuck Feeney's commitment to honouring his pledges and agreements, such as the Giving Pledge, underscored his dedication to philanthropy and his determination to inspire others to follow suit.

Chuck Feeney's philanthropic strategies were characterised by a blend of pragmatism, vision, and humility. His approach serves as an enduring example of how strategic giving, collaboration, and a relentless focus on impact can drive positive change in the world.

CHAPTER 6:The Secret Billionaire:

Chuck Feeney earned the nickname "The Secret Billionaire" for his extraordinary commitment to philanthropy coupled with his unwavering dedication to remaining anonymous and living a frugal lifestyle. Here's an exploration of why Chuck Feeney became known as "The Secret Billionaire":

1. Anonymous Giving:

Chuck Feeney's most distinctive characteristic was his dedication to anonymity in his philanthropic endeavours. He actively avoided personal recognition for his donations, often giving under the radar or through anonymous foundations.

2. Modest Lifestyle:

Feeney's personal life was characterised by frugality and simplicity. Despite being a billionaire, he chose to live a modest lifestyle, often flying economy class and staying in budget accommodations.

3. Minimalist Attire:

He was known for his minimalist attire, often seen wearing simple clothing and eschewing expensive accessories. This was in stark contrast to the ostentatious lifestyles of many other billionaires.

4. Humble Beginnings:

Feeney's upbringing and early life experiences played a significant role in shaping his desire to remain anonymous. He hailed from a working-class family and understood the importance of humility and giving back.

5. Focus on Impact, Not Recognition:

Feeney's primary concern was making a positive impact on the world, not gaining personal recognition. He believed that the causes he supported were more important than his name being associated with them.

6. Privacy as a Core Value:

Privacy was a core value for Chuck Feeney. He believed that personal wealth should not define an individual and that privacy allowed him to make decisions solely based on philanthropic impact.

7. Challenging the Status Quo:

Feeney's decision to remain anonymous challenged the prevailing norms of philanthropy, where many donors seek recognition and naming rights. His approach inspired a new generation of philanthropists to prioritise impact over personal acclaim.

8. Inspiring Others:

The mystery surrounding "The Secret Billionaire" inspired curiosity and admiration. His anonymity encouraged others to consider the profound impact of giving without seeking public acknowledgment.

9. The Unveiling of His Secret:

In 1997, Chuck Feeney's identity as "The Secret Billionaire" was revealed, but he continued to give anonymously. His secret was unveiled due to legal and regulatory requirements related to his philanthropic activities.

10. A Quiet Legacy:

Despite his anonymity, Chuck Feeney's philanthropic legacy is anything but quiet. His generosity and dedication to making the world a better place continue to inspire individuals and philanthropists worldwide.

Chuck Feeney's decision to be "The Secret Billionaire" was a testament to his commitment to philanthropy's core principles: humility, impact, and selflessness. His story serves as a reminder that true philanthropy is about giving to benefit others, not about personal recognition or wealth accumulation.Chuck Feeney's philanthropic journey left behind a remarkable and enduring legacy—one that is often described as "A Quiet Legacy." While his approach to giving was characterised by anonymity and humility, the impact of his philanthropy resonates loudly across the world. Here's a closer look at the quiet yet powerful legacy of Chuck Feeney:

1. Transforming Education:

One of the cornerstones of Chuck Feeney's philanthropy was his commitment to education. His donations to universities and schools have transformed educational institutions, expanded access to education, and empowered countless individuals to pursue their dreams.

2. Advancing Healthcare:

Feeney's contributions to healthcare and medical research have led to groundbreaking discoveries and improved healthcare services. His philanthropy has saved lives and improved the quality of healthcare for communities around the world.

3. Championing Social Justice:

Chuck Feeney's philanthropy extended to supporting organisations and initiatives that championed social justice. His contributions have advanced causes related to civil rights, human rights, and the fight against discrimination and inequality.

4. Influencing Philanthropy:

Feeney's "giving while living" philosophy has influenced the philanthropic landscape. His dedication to direct and high-impact giving inspired other billionaires to rethink their own philanthropic strategies, contributing to a shift in the sector.

5. Encouraging Anonymity:

His commitment to anonymity encouraged other philanthropists to consider a more low-profile approach to giving. This shift has allowed resources to flow to causes without overshadowing their importance.

6. Fostering Collaboration:

Chuck Feeney's collaborative approach to philanthropy set a precedent for partnerships between philanthropists, governments, and organisations. His willingness to work together for greater impact has inspired collective efforts.

7. Closing of The Atlantic Philanthropies:

The quiet closure of The Atlantic Philanthropies in 2020 marked the completion of Chuck Feeney's mission. This final act demonstrated his commitment to his vision and his desire to fulfil his philanthropic goals.

8. Inspiring Future Generations:

Perhaps the most enduring aspect of Chuck Feeney's legacy is the inspiration he provides to future generations of philanthropists and changemakers. His story challenges individuals to consider how they can make a difference in their lifetimes.

9. A Testament to Selflessness:

Chuck Feeney's legacy is a testament to selflessness and the idea that personal wealth can be a force for good. His life's work serves as a reminder that the true impact of philanthropy lies not in personal recognition but in the positive change it brings about.

10. Leaving a Better World:

Ultimately, Chuck Feeney's "A Quiet Legacy" stands as evidence that one person's dedication and determination can leave the world profoundly better than they found it. His story inspires individuals to think about the legacy they wish to leave behind.

Chuck Feeney's quiet legacy exemplifies the transformative power of philanthropy when driven by a deep commitment to making the world a better place. His influence continues to shape the way individuals and organisations approach giving, emphasising impact, humility, and the pursuit of a more just and equitable world.

6.1:The Remarkable Secrecy Surrounding Feeney's Philanthropy:

The remarkable secrecy surrounding Chuck Feeney's philanthropy was one of the most intriguing aspects of his charitable journey. Often referred to as "The Secret Billionaire," Feeney's commitment to anonymity added a unique layer to his philanthropic legacy. Here's a closer look at the extraordinary secrecy surrounding his giving:

1. Anonymous Donations:

   Chuck Feeney was known for making large donations to causes and organisations without attaching his name to them. He intentionally remained anonymous, allowing the impact of his giving to speak for itself.

2. Undercover Philanthropy:

   Feeney's approach to philanthropy was akin to undercover work. He went to great lengths to keep his giving hidden from public scrutiny, often using intermediary organisations to conceal the source of funds.

3. Humility Over Recognition:

   Rather than seeking personal recognition, Feeney prioritised humility. He believed that the causes he supported were more important than his name being associated with them.

4. Unveiling the Secret:

For decades, the identity of "The Secret Billionaire" remained unknown to the public. His anonymity was only revealed in 1997, when legal and regulatory requirements forced the disclosure of his philanthropic activities.

5. Low-Profile Lifestyle:

Feeney's personal lifestyle was intentionally low-profile and modest. He lived frugally, opting for economy class travel and budget accommodations, further shielding him from the public eye.

6. Meticulous Secrecy:

Feeney and his team were meticulous in maintaining secrecy. They employed legal and financial strategies to ensure that the details of his donations remained confidential.

7. Impact-Driven Giving:

The secrecy surrounding Feeney's giving allowed him to prioritise impact above all else. He made decisions based on where his resources could create the most significant positive change.

8. Legacy of Anonymous Giving:

Even after his anonymity was unveiled, Chuck Feeney continued to give anonymously. His legacy as "The Secret Billionaire" remains intact, serving as a testament to his commitment to causes over personal recognition.

9. Inspiring Others:

Feeney's secrecy inspired curiosity and admiration. His philanthropic journey challenged conventional norms and encouraged others to consider the importance of anonymity in giving.

10. Philanthropy Beyond Ego:

Chuck Feeney's approach to secrecy emphasised that philanthropy could transcend ego and personal acclaim. It underscored the notion that true philanthropy should be about creating positive change, not seeking recognition.

The remarkable secrecy surrounding Chuck Feeney's philanthropy added a layer of mystique to his giving, sparking fascination and intrigue. His dedication to keeping his identity hidden while creating profound impact exemplifies the idea that the true essence of philanthropy lies in the positive change it brings about, rather than the spotlight it attracts.

6.2:Legacy of Anonymous Giving:

Chuck Feeney's legacy of anonymous giving is a testament to the profound impact one person can have when driven by a commitment to philanthropy that transcends personal recognition. His deliberate choice to remain anonymous while generously donating billions of dollars to causes across the world leaves behind a unique and enduring legacy:

1. Philanthropy's Best-Kept Secret:

Chuck Feeney's philanthropy was one of the best-kept secrets for many years. He actively concealed his identity, allowing the impact of his giving to take precedence over personal recognition.

2. Focus on Impact:

Feeney's anonymity allowed him to focus solely on the impact of his donations rather than on the attention and acclaim that often accompany philanthropy. His giving was driven by a genuine desire to make the world a better place.

3. Inspiring Humility:

By choosing anonymity, Feeney demonstrated a remarkable level of humility. His actions inspired individuals and other philanthropists to prioritise the causes they supported over personal ego or recognition.

4. Influencing the Sector:

Chuck Feeney's legacy of anonymous giving influenced the philanthropic sector as a whole. It prompted a reevaluation of the role of personal recognition in philanthropy and encouraged other donors to consider more modest approaches.

5. A Quiet Example:

Feeney's legacy serves as a quiet yet powerful example of how philanthropy can create lasting change without fanfare. His story reminds us that the impact of giving should be at the forefront of any charitable endeavour.

6. Humanitarian Approach:

His anonymity underscored a humanitarian approach to philanthropy. Feeney believed in giving for the sake of helping others rather than for personal glory or recognition.

7. A Global Legacy:

Chuck Feeney's philanthropic reach extended across the globe. His donations have touched countless lives and left an indelible mark on education, healthcare, social justice, and scientific research worldwide.

8. A Lesson in Selflessness:

Feeney's legacy teaches us the value of selflessness in philanthropy. He showed that true generosity is about giving without expecting anything in return, not even recognition.

9. The Closing of The Atlantic Philanthropies:**
The closure of The Atlantic Philanthropies in 2020 marked the final chapter in Chuck Feeney's mission. It was a testament to his commitment to his vision and to the idea that philanthropy should focus on impact rather than perpetuity.

10. A Lasting Inspiration:
Perhaps Chuck Feeney's greatest legacy of anonymous giving is the inspiration it continues to provide. His story inspires others to give generously, quietly, and with a singular focus on creating positive change in the world.

Chuck Feeney's legacy of anonymous giving challenges us to rethink the role of recognition in philanthropy and underscores the profound impact that can be achieved when generosity is guided by a selfless commitment to improving the lives of others. His legacy will continue to inspire future generations of philanthropists to prioritise impact over personal acclaim.

6.3:A Lesson in Selflessness:

Chuck Feeney's life and philanthropic journey serve as a profound lesson in selflessness, demonstrating how one individual's dedication to giving can shape the world and inspire countless others. Here's an exploration of the valuable lesson in selflessness that Chuck Feeney's life imparts:

1. Prioritising Impact Over Recognition:

One of the most powerful lessons from Chuck Feeney's life is his unwavering commitment to prioritising the impact of his giving over personal recognition. He showed that true philanthropy is about helping others, not about seeking praise or fame.

2. Humility in Action:

Feeney's humility was on full display, not only in his giving but also in his modest lifestyle. He lived a simple, unassuming life, and his humility was a reflection of his dedication to his cause, not himself.

3. Giving While Living:

Chuck Feeney's "giving while living" philosophy was a lesson in selflessness. He recognized that the urgent needs of society required immediate action, and he dedicated his wealth to addressing those needs during his lifetime.

4. Inspiring Others:

Feeney's selfless approach to philanthropy has inspired countless individuals and philanthropists to rethink their giving. His example challenges others to consider how they can make a difference by focusing on the well-being of others.

5. Modest Lifestyle:

Despite being a billionaire, Feeney lived a modest life and practised what he preached. His minimalistic lifestyle was a testament to his selflessness and his belief in the value of a simple existence.

6. The Power of Anonymity:

Chuck Feeney's choice to remain anonymous emphasised the lesson that selflessness in giving can be more impactful when it doesn't seek personal recognition. His legacy shows that humility and generosity can be transformative.

7. A Legacy of Impact:

Perhaps the most profound lesson in selflessness is the legacy that Chuck Feeney leaves behind. His impact on education, healthcare, social justice, and more is a lasting testament to the positive change that can result from selfless giving.

8. Promoting Collaborative Philanthropy:

Feeney's selflessness extended to encouraging collaboration among philanthropists and organisations.

He believed in the power of working together to achieve greater impact, emphasising the common good over individual glory.

9. The Joy of Giving:

Chuck Feeney's life and actions underscore the joy that can be found in giving selflessly. He exemplified that true fulfilment comes from making a positive difference in the lives of others.

10. A Legacy of Inspiration:

Chuck Feeney's lesson in selflessness continues to inspire individuals to think beyond themselves and consider the impact they can have on the world. His legacy challenges us to embrace a selfless approach to philanthropy and to make giving an expression of compassion and empathy.

Chuck Feeney's lesson in selflessness is a reminder that philanthropy is not about the giver; it's about the beneficiaries and the positive change that can be achieved. His life and legacy inspire us to pursue selfless acts of generosity and work toward a world where the welfare of others is our primary focus.

6.4:The Billionaire Who Lived Frugally:

Chuck Feeney, often referred to as "The Billionaire Who Lived Frugally," was an exceptional example of how wealth and personal lifestyle choices can be at odds with one another. His story serves as a powerful testament to living a modest, unpretentious life despite immense wealth. Here's an exploration of this intriguing aspect of Chuck Feeney's life:

1. A Contradiction of Wealth:
   Chuck Feeney's modest lifestyle stood in stark contrast to his immense wealth. Despite being a billionaire, he chose to live frugally, embodying the idea that personal wealth doesn't have to dictate one's lifestyle.

2. An Unassuming Appearance:

Feeney's appearance was far from what one might expect of a billionaire. He was known for his minimalist attire, often wearing simple, unassuming clothing that didn't draw attention to his wealth.

3. Economy Class Travel:

Rather than flying in luxury, Feeney regularly opted for economy class when travelling. This was a clear departure from the extravagant travel habits of many other wealthy individuals.

4. Budget Accommodations:

He was frequently seen staying in budget accommodations, further emphasising his commitment to a frugal lifestyle. These choices demonstrated that comfort and luxury weren't his priorities.

5. A Lesson in Humility:

Chuck Feeney's frugality was a lesson in humility. He recognized that personal wealth should not define an individual, and he lived out this principle in his everyday life.

6. A Focus on Philanthropy:

By choosing to live frugally, Feeney was able to allocate a significant portion of his wealth to philanthropy. His modest lifestyle allowed him to give generously to causes he believed in.

7. Challenging Stereotypes:

His frugal lifestyle challenged the stereotypes associated with billionaires, who are often perceived as indulging in luxury. Feeney's choices showed that personal values can take precedence over material wealth.

8. Personal Contentment:

Chuck Feeney's frugal living demonstrated that personal contentment and happiness could be found in simplicity and selflessness, rather than in extravagant displays of affluence.

9. A Model for Others:

Feeney's modest lifestyle serves as a model for others to reconsider their own spending habits and priorities. It shows that living within one's means and embracing frugality can lead to a more fulfilling life.

10. A Lasting Legacy:

The billionaire who lived frugally leaves behind a lasting legacy, not only for his philanthropy but also as a reminder that personal values and principles can guide one's life, regardless of financial status.

Chuck Feeney's frugal lifestyle was not merely an anomaly but a deliberate choice based on his deeply held values. It challenges conventional notions about wealth and offers a compelling example of how living in alignment with one's principles can lead to personal contentment and the capacity to make a meaningful impact on the world.

CHAPTER 7:Philanthropy's Endgame:

Chuck Feeney's philanthropy had a clear and deliberate endgame that set him apart in the world of charitable giving. His approach, often referred to as "giving while living," was marked by the goal of donating his entire fortune to causes he cared about during his lifetime. Here's an exploration of Chuck Feeney's philanthropy endgame:

1. Giving While Living:

Chuck Feeney's endgame was centred around "giving while living." He was committed to using his wealth to address urgent societal needs during his lifetime rather than accumulating assets for future generations.

2. A Well-Defined Timeline:

Feeney set a specific timeline for his philanthropic activities. He believed in completing his giving mission by a certain date, which added a sense of urgency to his efforts.

3. Closing of The Atlantic Philanthropies:

The closing of The Atlantic Philanthropies in 2020 marked the culmination of Chuck Feeney's endgame. He had accomplished his mission of donating his entire fortune to various causes, resulting in the organisation's closure.

4. Mission Accomplished:

The fulfilment of his philanthropic endgame was a testament to his unwavering commitment to his values and the causes he supported. It demonstrated that he had achieved his objectives of making a significant impact on the world.

5. Emphasis on Impact:

Feeney's philanthropy was always focused on impact. His endgame was about creating real, positive change in areas such as education, healthcare, social justice, and scientific research.

6. Inspiring Other Philanthropists:

   Chuck Feeney's endgame has inspired other philanthropists to consider the impact of their giving and the benefits of allocating their wealth to pressing issues during their lifetimes.

7. A Legacy of Prioritising Urgent Needs

   His philanthropy endgame prioritised addressing urgent societal needs over perpetuating wealth. It emphasised that philanthropy should be responsive to the immediate challenges of the world.

8. A Shift in Philanthropic Norms:

   Feeney's endgame represented a shift in philanthropic norms. It challenged the conventional idea of amassing wealth for future generations and underscored the notion that personal wealth could be a force for good in the present.

9. Humility and Anonymity:

Even as he neared the fulfilment of his philanthropic endgame, Feeney continued to live humbly and anonymously. He didn't seek personal recognition for his contributions.

10. The Legacy of a Complete Life:

Chuck Feeney's philanthropy endgame exemplifies the idea that a life well-lived can be one that is dedicated to the betterment of others. His legacy is a testament to the profound impact that an individual can have through a selfless and focused approach to giving.

Chuck Feeney's philanthropy endgame not only transformed the lives of countless individuals but also challenged the conventions of wealth accumulation and demonstrated the profound influence of a committed individual in addressing the world's most pressing issues. His story inspires others to consider how they can make the most significant impact during their own lifetimes.The legacy of Chuck Feeney can be described as "The Legacy of a Complete Life." His journey of giving, selflessness, and purposeful philanthropy exemplifies how one individual's life can be not only fulfilling but also leave a lasting impact on the world. Here's an exploration of the legacy of a complete life that Chuck Feeney has bequeathed to us:

1. A Life of Purpose:

Chuck Feeney's legacy embodies a life of purpose. His philanthropic journey was driven by a deep commitment to making the world a better place, emphasising that true fulfillment comes from a life dedicated to meaningful goals.

2. The Joy of Giving:

Feeney's legacy reminds us of the joy that comes from giving and making a difference in the lives of others. His selfless approach to philanthropy illustrated the happiness that can be found in helping those in need.

3. A Complete Giving Mission:

Chuck Feeney's legacy is marked by the accomplishment of his philanthropic mission. He fulfilled his commitment to donate his entire fortune to various causes during his lifetime, closing The Atlantic Philanthropies in 2020.

4. An Inspiration to Others:

His complete life has served as an inspiration to countless individuals, philanthropists, and future generations. It challenges us to consider how we can make the most of our lives by prioritising the welfare of others.

5. Urgency and Impact:

Chuck Feeney's legacy underscores the importance of addressing urgent societal needs. His life was dedicated to creating tangible and immediate positive change in areas such as education, healthcare, and social justice.

6. A Shifting Philanthropic Paradigm:

His legacy reflects a paradigm shift in philanthropy, with a focus on "giving while living" rather than accumulating wealth for future generations. It encourages philanthropists to consider the impact they can have during their lifetimes.

7. A Lasting Mark on Education:

Feeney's complete life has left a profound impact on the field of education. His generous contributions have transformed educational institutions, expanded access to learning, and empowered countless individuals to pursue their dreams.

8. Emphasis on Anonymity:

Even as his life's mission was nearing completion, Feeney continued to live a modest and anonymous life, emphasising that humility should be at the core of philanthropy.

9. A Challenge to Conventions:

Chuck Feeney's complete life challenges the conventions of wealth accumulation and shows that personal wealth can be a powerful force for good in the present, rather than being hoarded for future generations.

10. The Legacy of a Philanthropic Giant:

Chuck Feeney's complete life leaves behind a legacy that demonstrates the incredible influence of an individual who dedicates their life to the well-being of others. It serves as a testament to the impact that can be achieved through selflessness and purpose-driven giving.

The legacy of a complete life that Chuck Feeney has left us serves as a reminder that our own lives can be most fulfilling when we strive for a sense of purpose and dedicate our efforts to improving the world for others. His story inspires us to consider how we, too, can make a meaningful impact during our lifetimes.

7.1:The Final Contributions:

Chuck Feeney's final contributions in the world of philanthropy marked the culmination of his extraordinary lifetime of giving. As he approached the completion of his philanthropic journey, these final acts of generosity held great significance and left a profound impact. Here's an exploration of Chuck Feeney's final contributions:

1. Closing of The Atlantic Philanthropies:
   The most significant of Chuck Feeney's final contributions was the closure of The Atlantic Philanthropies in 2020. This marked the completion of his mission to give away his entire fortune during his lifetime.

2. A Self-Imposed Deadline:
   Feeney's decision to close his philanthropic organisation was a testament to his self-imposed deadline. He had set a specific end date for his giving mission, emphasising the urgency of addressing pressing global issues.

3. A Symbol of Dedication:
   The closing of The Atlantic Philanthropies symbolised Chuck Feeney's unwavering dedication to his values and the causes he supported. It demonstrated that he had

accomplished his objectives of making a significant impact on the world.

4. Impact on Education:

One of his final contributions was a significant donation to Cornell University, where he had funded numerous projects over the years. This final act highlighted his enduring commitment to education and his desire to continue fostering learning.

5. The Importance of Completing the Mission:

Feeney's final contributions reinforced the importance of completing a philanthropic mission. It showcased his belief that personal wealth should be used to address immediate societal needs and not perpetuated.

6. Inspiring Future Generations:

His final acts of giving served as an inspiration to future generations of philanthropists. It showed that one individual, through determination and selflessness, could make a substantial impact on the world.

7. A Reminder of the "Giving While Living" Philosophy:

Chuck Feeney's final contributions were a reminder of his "giving while living" philosophy. They exemplified the idea that personal wealth can be a powerful force for good when allocated to address pressing issues during one's lifetime.

8. The Legacy of Urgency:

These final contributions emphasized the urgency with which Chuck Feeney approached his giving. His legacy challenges others to consider the immediate needs of society and the impact they can make in the present.

9. Anonymity and Humility:

Even in his final acts of giving, Chuck Feeney maintained his characteristic anonymity and humility. His choice to remain behind the scenes highlighted his unwavering commitment to the causes he supported.

10. A Philanthropic Giant's Closing Act:

The final contributions by Chuck Feeney were the closing act of a philanthropic giant. They serve as a reminder of the incredible influence of one individual who dedicated his life to the betterment of others.

Chuck Feeney's final contributions in the world of philanthropy demonstrated the profound impact that can be achieved when one's actions align with deeply held values and principles. His story continues to inspire us to consider how we, too, can make meaningful contributions to the world during our lifetimes.

7.2:Dissolution of The Atlantic Philanthropies:

The dissolution of The Atlantic Philanthropies marked a significant milestone in the remarkable philanthropic journey of Chuck Feeney. This act, which aligned with his principle of "giving while living," highlighted the importance of prioritising the urgent needs of society over personal wealth accumulation. Here's an exploration of the dissolution of The Atlantic Philanthropies:

1. The Closing Act of a Remarkable Journey:

The dissolution of The Atlantic Philanthropies was the final act in Chuck Feeney's extraordinary philanthropic journey. It symbolised the culmination of his mission to give away his entire fortune.

2. A Self-Imposed Deadline:

Feeney had set a specific deadline for the dissolution of his philanthropic organisation, demonstrating his commitment to completing his giving mission within his lifetime.

3. A Model for "Giving While Living":

The dissolution exemplified the "giving while living" philosophy, encouraging philanthropists to consider the immediate impact they can make by allocating their wealth to address pressing issues.

4. The Impact on Educational Institutions:

The Atlantic Philanthropies had a significant influence on educational institutions worldwide. Chuck Feeney's dissolution included substantial donations to universities and educational projects, reinforcing his lifelong commitment to learning and education.

5. Encouraging Collaboration:

The act of dissolving the organisation emphasised the importance of collaboration among philanthropists and organisations. Chuck Feeney believed in the power of working together to achieve greater impact.

6. The Power of Anonymity:

Even in the dissolution process, Chuck Feeney maintained his characteristic anonymity. His choice to give quietly underscored his focus on the causes he supported rather than personal recognition.

7. Philanthropy's Endgame:

The dissolution showcased the idea that philanthropy can have an endgame, where the wealth amassed over a lifetime is dedicated to creating lasting change rather than being hoarded.

8. The Legacy of Urgency:

Chuck Feeney's dissolution served as a reminder of the urgency with which he approached his philanthropy. His legacy challenges others to consider the immediate needs of society and the impact they can make during their lifetimes.

9. A Lasting Impact:

The dissolution of The Atlantic Philanthropies left behind a legacy of profound impact. The contributions made by the organisation continue to transform lives, institutions, and communities across the globe.

10. A Philanthropic Giant's Closing Chapter:

The dissolution of The Atlantic Philanthropies was the closing chapter in the philanthropic story of Chuck Feeney. It demonstrated that one individual, through selflessness, determination, and purpose-driven giving, could make an extraordinary impact on the world.

The dissolution of The Atlantic Philanthropies was not the end of Chuck Feeney's legacy but rather a powerful punctuation mark, reinforcing the idea that personal wealth, when allocated with purpose and urgency, can create significant, positive change. His philanthropic journey continues to inspire others to consider how they can make a meaningful difference during their own lifetimes.

7.3:The Legacy of Chuck Feeney's Giving:

The legacy of Chuck Feeney's giving is a profound testament to the transformative power of selflessness, determination, and impactful philanthropy. Over his lifetime, Feeney's generosity left an indelible mark on countless lives and organisations, and his legacy continues to inspire philanthropists and individuals around the world. Here's an exploration of the legacy of Chuck Feeney's giving:

1. Philanthropy as a Force for Good:

Chuck Feeney's legacy underscores the belief that personal wealth can be a powerful force for good. His life exemplified how philanthropy, when aligned with purpose and urgency, can drive positive change on a global scale.

2. The "Giving While Living" Philosophy:

Feeney's giving philosophy of "giving while living" challenges traditional notions of accumulating wealth for future generations. His legacy encourages philanthropists to consider the immediate needs of society and allocate resources accordingly.

3. Impact on Education:

Chuck Feeney's giving has had a profound impact on educational institutions worldwide. His support for learning and scholarship has expanded access to education and empowered countless individuals to pursue their dreams.

4. A Model of Anonymity and Humility:

His legacy is marked by a commitment to anonymity and humility. Feeney's giving was not about seeking personal recognition but about making a difference. His choice to remain behind the scenes is a lesson in selflessness.

5. Urgency in Philanthropy:

The urgency with which Feeney approached his giving is a central aspect of his legacy. His focus on addressing pressing issues of society underscores the importance of immediate action.

6. A Pioneer of Collaborative Philanthropy:

Chuck Feeney's legacy encourages collaborative philanthropy. He believed in the power of working together to achieve greater impact, emphasizing the common good over individual recognition.

7. Inspiring Future Generations:

His story is an enduring source of inspiration for philanthropists and individuals. It demonstrates that a single individual, through selflessness and determination, can make a profound and lasting impact.

8. The Legacy of a Complete Life:

Chuck Feeney's legacy exemplifies the idea of living a complete life. It encourages us to consider how we can make the most of our own lives by dedicating ourselves to causes that make a difference.

9. A Challenge to Conventional Norms:

His legacy challenges the conventional norms associated with wealth accumulation. It highlights the potential for personal wealth to be used as a force for immediate, positive change in the world.

10. A Philanthropic Giant's Enduring Impact:

The legacy of Chuck Feeney's giving is that of a philanthropic giant whose impact is felt around the world. His life serves as a reminder of the remarkable influence that one individual can have on society and future generations.

Chuck Feeney's giving legacy is a beacon of selflessness, determination, and purpose-driven philanthropy. His story continues to inspire us to consider how we can contribute to the betterment of the world and create a lasting impact in the lives of others.

7.4:Inspiring Future Generations:

Chuck Feeney's remarkable life of philanthropy continues to inspire future generations in numerous ways. His story serves as a beacon of selflessness, determination, and purpose-driven giving, encouraging individuals to make a positive impact on the world. Here's an exploration of how Chuck Feeney inspires future generations:

1. A Model of Generosity:

   Chuck Feeney's life demonstrates the profound impact of generosity. His willingness to give away his entire fortune during his lifetime sets an example of selflessness and the power of sharing one's wealth with those in need.

2. The "Giving While Living" Philosophy:

Feeney's commitment to "giving while living" challenges the conventional idea of accumulating wealth for future generations. It encourages philanthropists and individuals to consider the immediate needs of society and the impact they can make during their lifetimes.

3. Philanthropy as a Force for Good:

His legacy underscores the belief that personal wealth can be a powerful force for good. Chuck Feeney's life serves as a reminder that philanthropy, when aligned with purpose and urgency, can drive positive change on a global scale.

4. Embracing Anonymity and Humility:

Feeney's choice to remain anonymous and live a modest life demonstrates that philanthropy is not about seeking personal recognition but about making a difference. Future generations are inspired to prioritise impact over fame.

5. Urgency in Addressing Societal Issues:

The urgency with which Chuck Feeney approached his philanthropy highlights the importance of addressing pressing issues in society. His legacy encourages individuals to act promptly and decisively to create meaningful change.

6. Collaborative Philanthropy:

Feeney's legacy encourages collaborative philanthropy. He believed in the power of working together to achieve greater impact, emphasizing the common good over individual recognition. Future generations can learn from his emphasis on cooperation.

7. Leaving a Legacy of Impact:

His life demonstrates that a single individual, through selflessness and determination, can leave a legacy of profound impact. Future generations are inspired to consider how they, too, can make a lasting difference in the world.

8. Challenging Conventional Norms:

Chuck Feeney's legacy challenges the conventional norms associated with wealth accumulation. It encourages individuals to consider how personal wealth can be used as a force for immediate, positive change in the world.

9. Encouraging Humility and Modesty:
Future generations can learn from Feeney's modest lifestyle and his ability to live a simple, unpretentious life despite immense wealth. His example underscores the idea that personal values can take precedence over material wealth.

10. A Philanthropic Giant's Enduring Impact:
The enduring impact of Chuck Feeney's life inspires future generations to dream big and act selflessly. His story serves as a reminder that individuals have the potential to shape a better future for all.

Chuck Feeney's life of inspiring generosity and selflessness leaves a legacy that transcends generations. His story encourages individuals to consider how they can contribute to the betterment of the world and create a lasting impact in the lives of others, ensuring that his remarkable philanthropic spirit lives on.

CHAPTER 8:Impact on Society:

Chuck Feeney's impact on society is immeasurable, and his philanthropic contributions have left an enduring mark on numerous aspects of society. Through his selflessness, determination, and focused giving, he has significantly influenced various areas, inspiring change and bettering the lives of countless individuals. Here's an exploration of Chuck Feeney's impact on society:

1. Education and Learning:

Chuck Feeney's substantial contributions to education have expanded access to learning and scholarship. His support for educational institutions and projects has enabled individuals from diverse backgrounds to access quality education, thus empowering them to reach their full potential.

2. Healthcare Advancements:

His philanthropy has played a crucial role in advancing healthcare. By funding medical research, hospitals, and healthcare facilities, he has contributed to improved healthcare access and innovative medical solutions that benefit society at large.

3. Scientific and Medical Research:

Feeney's investments in scientific and medical research have led to breakthroughs in understanding diseases, developing new treatments, and enhancing the quality of life for those affected by various health conditions.

4. Social Justice and Equality:

Chuck Feeney's support for social justice initiatives and organisations has promoted equality and justice for marginalised and disadvantaged populations. His contributions have helped address systemic issues and create a fairer society.

5. Advancing Human Rights:

His philanthropy has supported human rights organisations and initiatives, contributing to the protection of human rights and freedoms globally. Feeney's impact extends to the promotion of democracy and the rule of law.

6. Inspiring Philanthropy:

Chuck Feeney's "giving while living" philosophy has inspired philanthropists to consider the immediate needs of society and the urgency of their giving. His approach to impactful philanthropy has encouraged others to focus on creating tangible and sustainable change.

7. Collaboration in Philanthropy:

His emphasis on collaborative philanthropy has fostered partnerships and cooperation among organisations and philanthropists. This collaborative spirit has led to greater synergy in addressing societal challenges.

8. Urgency in Addressing Pressing Issues:

Feeney's commitment to addressing urgent societal needs underscores the importance of acting promptly and decisively. His sense of urgency in philanthropy serves as a model for addressing pressing issues in society.

9. Philanthropy with Anonymity:

Chuck Feeney's dedication to anonymity and humility in philanthropy has shown that giving is about making a difference, not seeking personal recognition. His example has influenced how philanthropists approach their giving.

10. Challenging Conventional Norms:
Feeney's philanthropic approach challenges the conventional norms of wealth accumulation and inheritance. His legacy encourages a reconsideration of the impact of personal wealth on society and the potential for personal assets to be a force for immediate good.

Chuck Feeney's impact on society is a testament to the remarkable influence that one individual can have through selflessness and purpose-driven giving. His contributions have addressed urgent societal needs, fostered collaboration, and encouraged a sense of urgency in philanthropy, leaving a lasting legacy that continues to shape a better future for all.Chuck Feeney's commitment to advancing human rights is a testament to his deep belief in justice, equality, and the importance of protecting the fundamental rights of all individuals. Through his philanthropic efforts, he made significant contributions to organisations and initiatives dedicated to promoting and protecting human rights around the world. Here's an exploration of Chuck Feeney's impact on advancing human rights:

1. Supporting Advocacy and Awareness:

Feeney's philanthropy extended to organisations dedicated to raising awareness and advocating for human rights. His support played a vital role in bringing attention to critical issues, such as civil liberties, political freedoms, and the protection of vulnerable populations.

2. Defending Civil Liberties:

Chuck Feeney's contributions aided organisations that focused on defending civil liberties and individual freedoms. His support bolstered the efforts to protect the rights of individuals to express themselves, assemble peacefully, and seek justice.

3. Promoting Democracy and the Rule of Law:

Feeney recognized the importance of democratic governance and the rule of law. His philanthropic investments supported initiatives aimed at promoting and strengthening democratic processes and institutions, ultimately contributing to the protection of human rights.

4. Advancing Racial and Social Equality:

His support extended to organisations working to combat racial discrimination and social inequality. Feeney's contributions aimed to foster a more equitable and just society, where all individuals are treated with respect and dignity.

5. Protecting Vulnerable Populations:

Chuck Feeney's philanthropy included initiatives dedicated to protecting vulnerable populations, such as refugees, migrants, and displaced individuals. His support aided efforts to provide essential services, advocate for their rights, and address the challenges they face.

6. Fostering International Cooperation:

His contributions played a role in promoting international cooperation to protect human rights globally. Feeney's support facilitated collaboration among nations and organisations to address shared human rights concerns.

7. Encouraging a Culture of Rights:

Feeney's impact on human rights extends to fostering a culture of rights where individuals are aware of their rights and empowered to advocate for them. His contributions supported education and awareness programs to promote this culture.

8. A Commitment to Justice:

Chuck Feeney's philanthropy reflects a deep commitment to justice and the belief that all individuals should have access to a fair and impartial legal system. His support advanced initiatives that aimed to ensure access to justice for all.

9. Inspiring a Legacy of Human Rights Advocacy:

Chuck Feeney's lifelong dedication to human rights continues to inspire individuals and philanthropists to champion these essential causes. His legacy encourages others to uphold human rights as a fundamental part of a just and equitable society.

10. A Philanthropic Vision for a More Just World:

His contributions to human rights organisations and initiatives exemplify a philanthropic vision for a world where human rights are upheld, protected, and respected. Chuck Feeney's impact continues to shape the global conversation on human rights and justice.

Chuck Feeney's philanthropic efforts in advancing human rights demonstrate his unwavering commitment to creating a more just and equitable world. His legacy encourages individuals and organizations to continue the important work of protecting and promoting human rights for the benefit of all people.

8.1:Examining the Enduring Impact of Chuck Feeney's Philanthropy:

Examining the enduring impact of Chuck Feeney's philanthropy reveals a legacy of selflessness, determination, and transformative giving that has left an indelible mark on various aspects of society. His unwavering commitment to "giving while living" has inspired philanthropists and individuals around the world, and the effects of his generosity continue to shape the future. Here's a closer look at the enduring impact of Chuck Feeney's philanthropy:

1. Education and Learning:
   Feeney's contributions to education have paved the way for expanded access to learning and scholarship. His support for educational institutions and projects has empowered countless individuals to pursue higher education, unlocking opportunities for personal and societal growth.

2. Healthcare Advancements:

His philanthropic investments in healthcare have catalysed advancements in medical research, treatment, and patient care. The impact of his giving can be seen in improved healthcare access, innovative medical solutions, and enhanced quality of life for many.

3. Scientific and Medical Research:

Chuck Feeney's contributions to scientific and medical research have resulted in groundbreaking discoveries and innovative solutions for health-related challenges. The enduring legacy of his support continues to drive progress in these fields.

4. Social Justice and Equality:

Feeney's philanthropy has significantly contributed to social justice and equality. His support for initiatives and organisations working to combat discrimination and inequality has led to tangible improvements in societal fairness and justice.

5. Advancing Human Rights:

His contributions to human rights organisations and initiatives have had a lasting impact on the promotion and protection of fundamental freedoms and rights worldwide. Chuck Feeney's legacy underscores the importance of upholding human rights as a cornerstone of a just society.

6. Inspiring Philanthropy:

Feeney's philanthropic philosophy and approach have inspired philanthropists and individuals to adopt a "giving while living" mindset. His example encourages others to consider the urgency of philanthropy and its potential for immediate, meaningful change.

7. Collaboration in Philanthropy:

His emphasis on collaborative philanthropy has fostered partnerships and cooperation among organisations and philanthropists. This collaborative spirit continues to drive greater synergy and impact in addressing complex societal challenges.

8. Urgency in Addressing Pressing Issues:

Chuck Feeney's legacy serves as a reminder of the importance of addressing pressing societal issues with urgency. His approach encourages action in the present to create a better future for all.

9. Anonymity and Humility:

Feeney's dedication to anonymity and humility in his philanthropy sets an example of giving without seeking personal recognition. This enduring legacy highlights the impact that can be achieved when the focus is on the causes supported, not personal accolades.

10. Challenging Conventional Norms:

His philanthropic approach challenges the traditional norms of wealth accumulation and inheritance, advocating for the allocation of personal assets to address immediate societal needs. This shift in perspective continues to influence philanthropic discussions.

The enduring impact of Chuck Feeney's philanthropy is a testament to the remarkable influence that one individual can have on society through selflessness, determination, and a purpose-driven approach to giving. His legacy continues to inspire us to consider how we can contribute to the betterment of the world and create a lasting impact on the lives of others.

8.2:Social Justice and Equality:

Chuck Feeney's commitment to social justice and equality through his philanthropic efforts is a profound testament to his belief in a fair and just society for all. His generosity and unwavering support have left an enduring impact on numerous organisations and initiatives dedicated to promoting equality and combating discrimination. Here's an exploration of Chuck Feeney's impact on social justice and equality:

1. Supporting Equality Initiatives:
   Feeney's philanthropic contributions have played a pivotal role in supporting organisations and initiatives

that aim to address systemic inequalities and promote equality across various aspects of society.

2. Advancing Racial Equality:

His support extended to organisations focused on combatting racial discrimination and promoting racial equality. Chuck Feeney's contributions have fostered awareness and action to address racial disparities.

3. Advocating for Gender Equality:

Feeney recognized the importance of gender equality and women's rights. His philanthropy has aided organisations working to empower women, eliminate gender-based discrimination, and promote equal opportunities.

4. LGBTQ+ Rights:

Chuck Feeney's support has extended to LGBTQ+ rights organisations. His contributions have been instrumental in advocating for LGBTQ+ rights and fighting against discrimination based on sexual orientation and gender identity.

5. Promoting Inclusive Education:

His commitment to equality in education has supported initiatives aimed at making quality education accessible to all, regardless of socio-economic background, race, or gender.

6. Economic Equality and Poverty Alleviation:

Feeney's philanthropic investments have contributed to reducing economic inequality and alleviating poverty. His support for economic empowerment programs has enabled individuals to build better futures for themselves and their communities.

7. Inclusive Workforce Initiatives:

His support for initiatives promoting diversity and inclusivity in the workforce has encouraged equal employment opportunities for individuals of all backgrounds.

8. Advocacy for Criminal Justice Reform:

Chuck Feeney's contributions have been channelled into organisations advocating for criminal justice reform. His philanthropy has helped address issues related to mass incarceration and fairness in the legal system.

9. Fostering Dialogue and Understanding:
His legacy includes support for initiatives that foster dialogue and understanding between diverse communities and promote social harmony.

10. A Lifelong Commitment to Equality:
Chuck Feeney's philanthropy has demonstrated a lifelong commitment to the principles of social justice and equality. His legacy continues to inspire individuals and organisations to champion these causes.

Chuck Feeney's impact on social justice and equality transcends his lifetime, as his contributions continue to shape a more equitable and just world. His legacy encourages us to recognize the importance of equality and to work towards a society where all individuals are treated with respect, dignity, and fairness.Chuck

Feeney's lifelong commitment to equality is a remarkable testament to his unwavering dedication to creating a more just and equitable world. His philanthropic efforts spanned decades and were consistently guided by the principles of fairness and social justice. Here's an exploration of Chuck Feeney's enduring commitment to equality:

1. Early Recognition of Injustice:

From an early age, Chuck Feeney recognized the injustices and disparities that existed in society. His commitment to equality was rooted in a deep sense of empathy for those who faced discrimination and inequality.

2. Sustained Philanthropy:

Throughout his life, Feeney remained steadfast in his commitment to philanthropy that advanced equality. His giving was not a one-time act but a lifelong mission to address systemic disparities.

3. Diverse Causes and Initiatives:

Chuck Feeney's philanthropy covered a wide range of causes related to equality, including racial equality, gender equality, LGBTQ+ rights, and economic equality. His support touched the lives of countless individuals and communities.

4. Global Reach:

His commitment to equality extended beyond national borders. Feeney's philanthropy had a global impact, contributing to efforts that sought to combat discrimination and promote human rights worldwide.

5. Advocacy and Awareness:

Feeney's philanthropic support often included advocacy and awareness-building efforts. His contributions aided organisations that raised awareness about inequalities and advocated for policy changes to address them.

6. Inclusivity in Education:

His commitment to equality in education aimed at ensuring that quality learning opportunities were accessible to individuals from all walks of life, breaking down barriers that limited educational access.

7. Empowering Marginalised Communities:

Feeney's philanthropy empowered marginalised communities by supporting programs and initiatives that offered them the tools and resources to overcome obstacles and achieve equality.

8. Challenging Discrimination:

His lifelong commitment included supporting organisations that challenged discrimination in all its forms, be it based on race, gender, sexual orientation, or other factors.

9. Inclusive Workforce:

Feeney recognized the importance of a diverse and inclusive workforce. His philanthropy encouraged equal employment opportunities and inclusive workplace environments.

10. A Legacy of Equality:

Chuck Feeney's legacy is one of unwavering commitment to the principles of social justice and equality. His life's work continues to inspire individuals and organisations to carry forward the mission of promoting equality and justice for all.

Chuck Feeney's lifelong commitment to equality serves as a beacon of hope and inspiration. It reminds us that individuals can make a profound difference in the world by dedicating themselves to the causes of fairness, justice, and equality. His legacy challenges us to continue the ongoing work of creating a society where every individual is treated with respect, dignity, and the opportunity to thrive.

8.3:Challenging Discrimination:

Chuck Feeney's philanthropic efforts were marked by his unwavering commitment to challenging discrimination in all its forms. His contributions and support extended to organisations and initiatives dedicated to addressing and combatting discrimination. Here's an exploration of Chuck Feeney's impact in challenging discrimination:

1. Racial Equality:

Feeney's philanthropy included substantial support for organisations and initiatives working to eliminate racial discrimination. His contributions were instrumental in raising awareness about the systemic disparities faced by minority communities and advocating for racial equality.

2. Gender Equality:

Chuck Feeney recognized the importance of gender equality and women's rights. His philanthropic investments supported organisations and projects that aimed to empower women, eliminate gender-based discrimination, and create equal opportunities for all genders.

3. LGBTQ+ Rights:

His support extended to LGBTQ+ rights organisations. Feeney's contributions have played a significant role in advocating for LGBTQ+ rights, combating discrimination based on sexual orientation and gender identity, and promoting inclusivity.

4. Disability Rights:

Feeney's commitment to challenging discrimination also extended to supporting organisations focused on advocating for the rights and inclusion of individuals with disabilities. His philanthropy aimed to create a more accessible and equal world for everyone.

5. Age Discrimination:

His philanthropy recognized the importance of combating age discrimination. Feeney's support aided initiatives that aimed to address stereotypes and biases related to age, ensuring that individuals of all ages have equal opportunities.

6. Advocating for Equal Opportunities:

Feeney's contributions were often directed at initiatives that advocated for equal opportunities in education, employment, and access to essential services, ensuring that individuals faced no discrimination based on their background or characteristics.

7. Access to Justice:

His philanthropic support also played a crucial role in improving access to justice for individuals who faced discrimination. Chuck Feeney's contributions aided organisations that provided legal representation and advocacy for those who experienced discrimination.

8. Promoting Diversity and Inclusion:

His lifelong commitment encouraged diversity and inclusion in all aspects of society, from workplaces to communities. His support contributed to building more diverse and inclusive environments where discrimination was challenged.

9. A Legacy of Tolerance and Acceptance:

Chuck Feeney's legacy is one of promoting tolerance and acceptance. His contributions continue to challenge discriminatory practices, fostering a more inclusive and equitable society.

10. A Call to Action:

Chuck Feeney's philanthropic efforts serve as a call to action for individuals and organisations to join the fight against discrimination. His legacy reminds us that we all have a role to play in creating a world free from discrimination and inequality.

Chuck Feeney's dedication to challenging discrimination is a testament to his enduring commitment to fairness, justice, and equality. His philanthropy has left a lasting impact on the organisations and initiatives that continue the vital work of combating discrimination in all its forms. His legacy encourages us to stand up against discrimination and advocate for a more equitable and inclusive world.

8.4:Lessons for Aspiring Philanthropists:

Chuck Feeney's life and philanthropic journey offer invaluable lessons for aspiring philanthropists and individuals who wish to make a positive impact on the world. His "giving while living" philosophy, humility, and commitment to creating a better society provide inspiration and guidance for those who seek to follow in his footsteps. Here are some key lessons from Chuck Feeney's philanthropic legacy:

1. "Giving While Living":

One of Chuck Feeney's most profound lessons is the concept of "giving while living." He exemplified the idea that philanthropy should address urgent needs, and resources should be directed to create positive change during one's lifetime.

2. Humility and Anonymity:

Feeney's commitment to giving without seeking recognition teaches us the importance of humility in philanthropy. His anonymous approach emphasises that the focus should be on the causes supported, not personal accolades.

3. Collaborative Philanthropy:

Chuck Feeney's emphasis on collaborative philanthropy highlights the value of partnerships and cooperation among organisations and philanthropists. Collaborative efforts often result in greater impact and more efficient solutions to complex problems.

4. Urgency in Philanthropy:

Feeney's sense of urgency underscores the importance of acting promptly to address pressing societal issues. Aspiring philanthropists should recognize that time is of the essence in making a meaningful difference.

5. Focus on Systemic Change:

His philanthropy addressed the root causes of social issues, advocating for systemic change rather than mere band-aid solutions. Aspiring philanthropists can follow this lesson by aiming for long-term impact.

6. Diverse Philanthropic Causes:

Chuck Feeney's support spanned diverse causes, from education to healthcare, social justice, and human rights. Aspiring philanthropists can learn to be open to a wide range of issues and find where their passions align with pressing needs.

7. Giving Back to the Community:

 - Feeney's legacy highlights the significance of giving back to one's community and contributing to local initiatives that make a difference in people's lives.

8. Inspiring Others:

His lifetime of giving inspires others to adopt a philanthropic mindset. Aspiring philanthropists can draw motivation from his example to create their own meaningful legacies.

9. Challenges and Persistence:

Chuck Feeney faced challenges throughout his philanthropic journey, but his unwavering commitment and persistence allowed him to overcome obstacles. Aspiring philanthropists should be prepared for challenges and persevere in their mission.

10. A Legacy of Impact:

Lesson in impactful giving

Perhaps the most significant lesson is that individuals can leave a legacy of impact that endures beyond their lifetime. Aspiring philanthropists should aim to create a lasting legacy of positive change in the world.

Chuck Feeney's life and philanthropy serve as a beacon of inspiration for aspiring philanthropists. His lessons emphasise the importance of urgency, humility, collaboration, and long-term systemic change in philanthropy. Following his example can help individuals make a meaningful and enduring impact on the lives of others and society as a whole.

CHAPTER 9:Life Beyond Philanthropy:

Chuck Feeney's life went beyond his remarkable philanthropic endeavours. While his philanthropy was a central aspect of his identity, he had a life enriched by various interests and experiences. Here's a look at Chuck Feeney's life beyond philanthropy:

1. Entrepreneurial Success:

   Before embarking on his philanthropic journey, Chuck Feeney achieved considerable success as a co-founder of Duty-Free Shoppers (DFS). DFS became a global retail powerhouse, and his entrepreneurial spirit played a significant role in his life.

2. Friendship and Partnerships:

   His enduring friendship and partnership with Robert W. Miller, with whom he co-founded DFS, were a crucial part of his life. Their business ventures laid the foundation for his philanthropic journey.

3. Passion for Travel:

Given his involvement in the travel retail industry, Chuck Feeney had a deep appreciation for travel. This passion allowed him to explore the world and develop a global perspective, which informed his philanthropic decisions.

4. A Frugal Lifestyle:

Feeney's personal life was marked by a frugal lifestyle. He chose to live modestly and use resources responsibly. This simplicity was a reflection of his values and commitment to making the most of his wealth for philanthropic causes.

5. Family and Loved Ones:

Chuck Feeney cherished his family and close relationships. His personal life revolved around loved ones, and he maintained a strong bond with those who were dear to him.

6. Retirement:

In his later years, he announced his retirement from active philanthropy, aligning with the principles of the Giving Pledge. His retirement allowed him to reflect on a life rich in experiences and a profound legacy of giving.

7. Legacy of Inspiration:

Beyond his financial wealth, Chuck Feeney's life served as a source of inspiration for countless individuals. His commitment to "giving while living" encouraged others to reflect on their own lives and the impact they can make on the world.

8. Recognition and Awards:

While he preferred to remain anonymous in his giving, Chuck Feeney received various awards and honours in acknowledgment of his philanthropic contributions. These recognitions added to the tapestry of his life.

9. Commitment to Secrecy:

Chuck Feeney's commitment to anonymity and secrecy in his personal life was consistent with his approach to philanthropy. He valued discretion, believing that the focus should be on the causes he supported rather than his personal story.

10. A Life Well Lived:

Chuck Feeney's life, both within and beyond philanthropy, was a life well lived. His experiences, relationships, and unwavering dedication to making a difference are a testament to the transformative power of one individual's commitment to the greater good.

Chuck Feeney's life beyond philanthropy demonstrated that a person's impact goes beyond financial contributions. It serves as a reminder that the choices we make, the relationships we nurture, and the values we uphold are integral parts of our legacies. His life was an embodiment of living with purpose and making a difference in the world.Chuck Feeney's life was indeed a testament to a life well lived. His journey, marked by humility, dedication, and a profound commitment to philanthropy, serves as an inspiring example of how one individual can make a lasting impact on the world.

Lesson in impactful giving

Here's an exploration of Chuck Feeney's life as one well lived:

1. A Legacy of Giving:

Chuck Feeney's life was characterised by a legacy of selfless giving. He committed to giving away his fortune during his lifetime, dedicating himself to addressing pressing global issues.

2. Humility and Anonymity:

Feeney's humility and anonymity were core principles of his life. He avoided personal recognition, choosing instead to direct attention to the causes he supported. His quiet approach to philanthropy set an extraordinary example.

3. Commitment to "Giving While Living":

One of the most profound aspects of Feeney's life was his unwavering commitment to "giving while living." He believed that philanthropy should address immediate needs, and he worked tirelessly to fulfil this commitment.

4. Modest Lifestyle:

Despite his substantial wealth, Chuck Feeney lived a notably modest lifestyle. He favoured simplicity, frugality, and responsible resource use, aligning his personal life with his philanthropic values.

5. An Entrepreneurial Journey:

Before his philanthropic endeavours, Chuck Feeney was a successful entrepreneur. His co-founding of Duty-Free Shoppers marked the beginning of a prosperous career that would ultimately serve as a foundation for his giving.

6. Inspiring Others:

Feeney's life inspired countless individuals, from aspiring philanthropists to those who admired his humility and dedication. He demonstrated that even one person's efforts can make a profound impact on the world.

7. Commitment to Social Justice:

His philanthropy was deeply rooted in his commitment to social justice and equality. He worked tirelessly to address systemic disparities and create a more just and equitable world.

8. Legacy of Impact:

Chuck Feeney's life left a legacy of significant impact. His contributions transformed education, healthcare, human rights, and social justice, touching the lives of countless individuals and communities.

9. Fulfilment of the Giving Pledge:

His commitment to fulfilling the Giving Pledge exemplified his dedication to philanthropy. It was a pledge he fulfilled with grace and determination, setting an example for future generations.

10. A Life of Purpose:

Above all, Chuck Feeney's life was a life of deep purpose. He found meaning in making the world a better place, and his journey exemplified how one individual's commitment and dedication can leave a profound and enduring legacy.

Chuck Feeney's life was not defined by material wealth but by the wealth of his dedication to improving the lives of others. His legacy serves as an enduring example of a life well lived, illustrating that one person's choices and actions can have a transformative impact on the world and inspire others to do the same.

9.1:Retirement:

Chuck Feeney's retirement marked a significant milestone in the life of a remarkable philanthropist. After decades of selfless giving and dedicated efforts to improve the world, he made the decision to retire from active philanthropy. Here's a closer look at Chuck Feeney's retirement:

1. The Quiet Exit:

Chuck Feeney chose to retire from active philanthropy in a characteristically modest and understated manner. His retirement was announced quietly and in keeping with his lifelong preference for anonymity.

2. The Fulfilment of the Giving Pledge:

Chuck Feeney's retirement aligns with the principles of the Giving Pledge, a commitment by some of the world's wealthiest individuals to give away the majority of their wealth during their lifetimes or in their wills. His fulfilment of this pledge was an inspiring testament to his dedication to "giving while living."

3. Sunsetting The Atlantic Philanthropies:

As part of his retirement, Feeney's foundation, The Atlantic Philanthropies, began a systematic process of winding down its operations. The foundation strategically allocated its remaining resources to complete ongoing projects and initiatives.

4. Legacy of Impact:

Chuck Feeney's retirement leaves a legacy of profound impact on education, healthcare, social justice, and human rights. His contributions have transformed countless lives and communities, and this legacy continues to inspire philanthropists worldwide.

5. Encouraging Others:

His retirement sends a powerful message to others, encouraging them to consider their philanthropic journeys and the impact they can make during their lifetimes. It emphasises the urgency of philanthropy in addressing pressing global issues.

6. A Humble Exit:

Chuck Feeney's retirement emphasises his lifelong commitment to humility and anonymity in philanthropy. Even in retirement, he maintained his focus on the causes he supported rather than seeking recognition.

7. Philanthropy's Role in Retirement:

His retirement highlights the role that philanthropy can play in individuals' lives after they've achieved financial success. It showcases how the act of giving can bring fulfilment and purpose to one's retirement years.

8. Lessons for the Next Generation:

Chuck Feeney's retirement serves as an enduring lesson for the next generation of philanthropists, demonstrating the positive impact that can be achieved by dedicating one's wealth and resources to meaningful causes.

9. Reflection on a Remarkable Journey:

His retirement provided an opportunity for reflection on the remarkable journey of a man who, through his lifetime of giving, inspired countless individuals to think differently about their wealth and its potential for positive change.

10. A Lifelong Commitment Realised:

Chuck Feeney's retirement represents the culmination of a lifelong commitment to "giving while living." His example serves as a model for individuals to consider how they can fulfil their philanthropic aspirations during their lifetimes.

Chuck Feeney's retirement from active philanthropy is a momentous chapter in the life of a man who dedicated himself to creating a more just and equitable world. His legacy continues to inspire individuals and philanthropists to follow his example and make a positive impact on the lives of others.

9.2:Personal Life:

Chuck Feeney's personal life was marked by a combination of humility, privacy, and a dedication to making a difference in the world through his philanthropic efforts. Despite his enormous wealth, he led a relatively modest and private life, often shying away from the public eye. Here's an overview of Chuck Feeney's personal life:

1. Humble Beginnings:

Lesson in impactful giving

Charles "Chuck" Francis Feeney was born on April 23, 1931, in Elizabeth, New Jersey, USA. He came from modest beginnings, which played a significant role in shaping his values and philanthropic outlook.

2. Educational Journey:

Feeney attended Cornell University, where he met Robert W. Miller, his future business partner. Together, they launched their first business ventures, setting the stage for his future success.

3. Duty-Free Shoppers (DFS):

In 1960, Feeney and Miller co-founded Duty-Free Shoppers (DFS), a chain of luxury retail stores catering to travellers. DFS became highly successful, contributing to Feeney's considerable wealth.

4. Commitment to Giving:

Despite accumulating vast wealth, Feeney made a deliberate choice to dedicate his fortune to philanthropy. He adopted a philosophy of "giving while living," committing to give away the majority of his wealth during his lifetime.

5. Anonymous Philanthropy:

One of the hallmarks of Chuck Feeney's personal life was his commitment to anonymous giving. He preferred to remain out of the public spotlight and gave discreetly, focusing on the impact rather than seeking recognition.

6. Family and Relationships:

Chuck Feeney was known for his close-knit family and cherished his relationships with loved ones. He maintained a private family life and kept his personal relationships away from the public eye.

7. Frugal Lifestyle:

Feeney's personal life was characterised by a notably frugal lifestyle. He opted for modest clothing, used public transportation, and lived in a simple apartment. His lifestyle aligned with his belief in the responsible use of resources.

8. Retirement:

In his later years, Chuck Feeney announced his retirement from active philanthropy. His retirement marked the fulfilment of his commitment to the Giving Pledge, a promise to give away the majority of his wealth during his lifetime.

9. Impact on Philanthropy:

Chuck Feeney's personal life, characterised by his humility, anonymity, and dedication to giving, left an enduring impact on philanthropy. He served as an example of how individuals can use their wealth to create meaningful change.

10. Legacy:

Chuck Feeney's personal life exemplified a deep sense of purpose and a commitment to leaving a lasting legacy of positive impact on society. His life's work continues to inspire individuals and philanthropists worldwide.

Chuck Feeney's personal life reflects a unique blend of humility, dedication, and a strong desire to make the world a better place. His commitment to "giving while living" and focus on the greater good serve as a powerful example for individuals seeking to lead meaningful and purpose-driven lives.

9.3:Reflecting on a Life of Purpose:

Reflecting on Chuck Feeney's life, one is confronted with a remarkable journey defined by purpose, humility, and an unwavering commitment to making a difference in the world. Chuck Feeney's story provides invaluable insights into the power of philanthropy and the profound impact that one individual can have on society. Here, we reflect on his life of purpose:

1. A Humble Beginning:
   Chuck Feeney's life began with humble roots, and it was his early experiences that instilled in him a deep sense of humility and a desire to help others.

2. A Vision for Impact:

As he ventured into entrepreneurship, he developed a vision for impact that went far beyond business success. His vision was rooted in the belief that wealth should be used to create positive change.

3. "Giving While Living":

  - Perhaps the most defining aspect of Chuck Feeney's life was his unwavering commitment to "giving while living." He believed in addressing pressing issues during his lifetime rather than leaving philanthropic decisions to others.

4. The Power of Anonymity:

  Feeney's choice to remain anonymous in his giving demonstrated that it's the causes and the impact that matter most. He focused on making a difference rather than seeking personal recognition.

5. Philanthropy's Urgency:

  His life emphasised the urgency of philanthropy. He recognized that the world's challenges required immediate action and that philanthropy should serve to effect change as soon as possible.

6. Wide-Ranging Impact:

Chuck Feeney's philanthropic efforts had a far-reaching impact. His contributions touched on diverse issues, from education and healthcare to social justice and human rights.

7. A Legacy of Transformation:

His life leaves behind a legacy of transformation. The institutions, organisations, and initiatives he supported continue to change lives and create a more equitable world.

8. Inspiring Others:

Chuck Feeney's life serves as an enduring source of inspiration for individuals and aspiring philanthropists, reminding them of the extraordinary impact that can be made through dedication and selfless giving.

9. Lessons for Future Generations:

His life imparts crucial lessons for future generations, emphasising the importance of acting with purpose, humility, and a commitment to addressing the world's most pressing issues.

10. A Life Well Lived:

Chuck Feeney's life was truly well lived. His journey exemplified how a life driven by purpose, philanthropy, and the greater good can leave a profound and lasting impact on the world.

Reflecting on Chuck Feeney's life of purpose is a reminder that each individual has the potential to make a meaningful and enduring impact. His legacy serves as a call to action, inspiring us to consider how we can contribute to positive change and make the world a better place, one selfless act at a time.

9.4:Lessons for Future Generations:

Chuck Feeney's life and philanthropic journey offer a wealth of lessons for future generations. His legacy serves as a source of inspiration and guidance for individuals seeking to make a positive impact on the world. Here are some essential lessons derived from Chuck Feeney's remarkable life:

1. "Giving While Living":

Chuck Feeney's commitment to "giving while living" teaches future generations the importance of addressing urgent global issues promptly. Waiting for one's wealth to be distributed posthumously may not have the same transformative impact.

2. Humility and Anonymity:

Feeney's choice to give anonymously underscores the significance of humility and the idea that the focus of philanthropy should be on the causes supported, not personal recognition.

3. Urgency in Philanthropy:

His life emphasises the urgency of philanthropic action. Future generations should recognize that the world's challenges require swift and effective responses.

4. Collaborative Philanthropy:

Chuck Feeney's emphasis on collaborative philanthropy highlights the value of partnerships and cooperation among organisations and philanthropists. Together, we can achieve greater impact.

5. Broad Philanthropic Interests:

Feeney's support for diverse causes, from education to healthcare and social justice, shows that future philanthropists should remain open to a wide range of issues and causes.

6. Modesty and Responsible Resource Use:

His frugal lifestyle exemplifies that wealth doesn't have to be flaunted. Future generations can learn to use resources responsibly, ensuring that philanthropic efforts are maximally effective.

7. Commitment to Social Justice:

Chuck Feeney's dedication to social justice teaches the importance of addressing systemic disparities and working toward a more just and equitable society.

8. Overcoming Challenges:

He faced numerous challenges on his philanthropic journey, but his persistence and commitment allowed him to overcome them. Future generations should be prepared to persevere in the face of obstacles.

9. Leaving a Legacy of Impact:

Perhaps the most significant lesson is that individuals have the potential to leave a lasting legacy of positive change. Future generations should aim to create enduring impact and transform lives.

10. Inspiration for Aspiring Philanthropists:

Chuck Feeney's life is an enduring source of inspiration for aspiring philanthropists. His journey illustrates that even one person's efforts can make a profound difference in the world.

In summary, Chuck Feeney's life and philanthropic philosophy emphasise the need for urgency, humility, collaboration, and a commitment to creating lasting impact. His legacy continues to inspire individuals and future generations to harness their resources and energies for the betterment of society.

CONCLUSION:

In conclusion, Chuck Feeney's life is a testament to the transformative power of philanthropy, humility, and a relentless commitment to making the world a better place. His legacy serves as an enduring source of inspiration and guidance for individuals, philanthropists, and society as a whole.

Chuck Feeney's journey was marked by several key principles:

1. "Giving While Living": He dedicated his wealth to addressing immediate global challenges, emphasising the importance of timely action in philanthropy.

2. Anonymity:His choice to give anonymously underscores the notion that true philanthropy is selfless and should focus on the greater good rather than personal recognition.

3. A Broad Philanthropic Vision: Chuck Feeney supported a wide range of causes, from education to healthcare, social justice, and human rights, reflecting his deep commitment to addressing diverse societal issues.

4. Frugality and Responsibility: His modest lifestyle demonstrated that wealth can be used responsibly, ensuring that philanthropic efforts have maximum impact.

5. Collaborative Philanthropy: His dedication to partnerships and cooperation exemplifies how collective efforts can achieve greater results.

6. Urgency in Philanthropy:He underscored the urgency of addressing pressing global issues, recognizing that the world's challenges require immediate action.

7. A Legacy of Impact: Chuck Feeney's life and work have left an indelible legacy, transforming countless lives and inspiring generations to come.

His life was not defined by material wealth, but by the wealth of his dedication to improving the lives of others. Chuck Feeney's legacy challenges us to consider how we can create a positive impact in the world, emphasising that each individual has the potential to make a difference, regardless of their means. His story reminds us that a life marked by purpose, humility, and selfless giving can leave a profound and enduring mark on society.